# Jean-Paul Sartre

# literature &
# existentialism

TRANSLATED FROM THE FRENCH
BY BERNARD FRECHTMAN

Citadel Press
Kensington Publishing Corp.
www.kensingtonbooks.com

CITADEL PRESS books are published by

Kensington Publishing Corp.
850 Third Avenue
New York, NY 10022

Originally published as *What Is Literature?*

All Kensington titles, imprints, and distributed lines are available at
special quantity discounts for bulk purchases for sales promotions,
premiums, fund raising, educational, or institutional use. Special book
excerpts or customized printings can also be created to fit specific
needs. For details, write or phone the office of the Kensington special
sales manager: Kensington Publishing Corp., 850 Third Avenue,
New York, NY 10022, attn: Special Sales Department,
phone 1-800-221-2647.

First printing 1991

20 19 18 17 16 15 14 13 12 11 10

Printed in the United States of America

ISBN 0–8065–0105–7

# TABLE OF CONTENTS

Foreword

# FOREWORD

*"If you want to engage yourself," writes a young imbecile, "what are you waiting for? Join the Communist Party." A great writer who engaged himself often and disengaged himself still more often, but who has forgotten, said to me, "The worst artists are the most engaged. Look at the Soviet painters." An old critic gently complained, "You want to murder literature. Contempt for belles-lettres is spread out insolently all through your review." A petty mind calls me pigheaded, which for him is evidently the highest insult. An author who barely crawled from one war to the other and whose name sometimes awakens languishing memories in old men accuses me of not being concerned with immortality; he knows, thank God, any number of people whose chief hope it is. In the eyes of an American hack-journalist the trouble with me is that I have not read Bergson or Freud; as for Flaubert, who did not engage himself, it seems that he haunts me like remorse. Smart-alecks wink at me, "And poetry? And painting? And music? You want to engage them, too?" And some martial spirits demand, "What's it all about? Engaged literature? Well, it's the old socialist realism, unless it's a revival of populism, only more aggressive."*

*What nonsense. They read quickly, badly, and pass judgment before they have understood. So let's begin all over. This doesn't amuse anyone, neither you nor me. But we have to hit the nail on the head. And since critics condemn me in the name of literature without ever saying what they mean by that, the best answer to give them is to examine the art of writing without prejudice. What is writing? Why does one write? For whom? The fact is, it seems that nobody has ever asked himself these questions.*

# I

## WHAT IS WRITING?

No, we do not want to "engage" painting, sculpture, and music "too," or at least not in the same way. And why would we want to? When a writer of past centuries expressed an opinion about his craft, was he immediately asked to apply it to the other arts? But today it's the thing to do to "talk painting" in the argot of the musician or the literary man and to "talk literature" in the argot of the painter, as if at bottom there were only one art which expressed itself indifferently in one or the other of these languages, like the Spinozistic substance which is adequately reflected by each of its attributes.

Doubtless, one could find at the origin of every artistic calling a certain undifferentiated choice which circumstances, education, and contact with the world particularized only later. Besides, there is no doubt that the arts of a period mutually influence each other and are conditioned by the same social factors. But those who want to expose the absurdity of a literary theory by showing that it is inapplicable to music must first prove that the arts are parallel.

Now, there is no such parallelism. Here, as everywhere, it is not only the form which differentiates, but the matter

7

as well. And it is one thing to work with color and sound, and another to express oneself by means of words. Notes, colors, and forms are not signs. They refer to nothing exterior to themselves. To be·sure, it is quite impossible to reduce them strictly to themselves, and the idea of a pure sound, for example, is an abstraction. As Merleau-Ponty has pointed out in *The Phenomenology of Perception,* there is no quality of sensation so bare that it is not penetrated with signification. But the dim little meaning which dwells within it, a light joy, a timid sadness, remains immanent or trembles about it like a heat mist; it *is* color or sound. Who can distinguish the green apple from its tart gaiety? And aren't we already saying too much in naming "the tart gaiety of the green apple?" There is green, there is red, and that is all. They are things, they exist by themselves.

It is true that one might, by convention, confer the value of signs upon them. Thus, we talk of the language of flowers. But if, after the agreement, white roses signify "fidelity" to me, the fact is that I have stopped seeing them as roses. My attention cuts through them to aim beyond them at this abstract virtue. I forget them. I no longer pay attention to their mossy abundance, to their sweet stagnant odor. I have not even perceived them. That means that I have not behaved like an artist. For the artist, the color, the bouquet, the tinkling of the spoon on the saucer, are *things,* in the highest degree. He stops at the quality of the sound or the form. He returns to it constantly and is enchanted with it. It is this color-object that he is going to transfer to his canvas, and the only modification he will make it undergo is that he will transform it into an *imaginary* object. He is therefore as far as he can be from considering colors and signs as a *language.*[1]

What is valid for the elements of artistic creation is also valid for their combinations. The painter does not want to create a thing.[2] And if he puts together red, yellow, and green, there is no reason for the ensemble to have a definable signification, that is, to refer particularly to another object. Doubtless this ensemble is also inhabited by a soul, and since there must have been motives, even hidden ones, for the painter to have chosen yellow rather than violet, it may be asserted that the objects thus created reflect his deepest tendencies. However, they never express his anger, his anguish, or his joy as do words or the expression of the face; they are impregnated with these emotions; and in order for them to have crept into these colors, which by themselves already had something like a meaning, his emotions get mixed up and grow obscure. Nobody can quite recognize them there.

Tintoretto did not choose that yellow rift in the sky above Golgotha to *signify* anguish or to *provoke* it. It is anguish and yellow sky at the same time. Not sky of anguish or anguished sky; it is an anguish become thing, an anguish which has turned into yellow rift of sky, and which thereby is submerged and impasted by the proper qualities of things, by their impermeability, their extension, their blind permanence, their externality, and that infinity of relations which they maintain with other things. That is, it is no longer *readable*. It is like an immense and vain effort, forever arrested half-way between sky

9

and earth, to express what their nature keeps them from expressing.

Similarly, the signification of a melody—if one can still speak of signification—is nothing outside of the melody itself, unlike ideas, which can be adequately rendered in several ways. Call it joyous or somber. It will always be over and above anything you can say about it. Not because its passions, which are perhaps at the origin of the invented theme, have, by being incorporated into notes, undergone a transubstantiation and a transmutation. A cry of grief is a sign of the grief which provokes it, but a song of grief is both grief itself and something other than grief. Or, if one wishes to adopt the existentialist vocabulary, it is a grief which does not *exist* any more, which *is*. But, you will say, suppose the painter does houses? That's just it. He *makes* them, that is, he creates an imaginary house on the canvas and not a sign of a house. And the house which thus appears preserves all the ambiguity of real houses.

The writer can guide you and, if he describes a hovel, make it seem the symbol of social injustice and provoke your indignation. The painter is mute. He presents you with *a* hovel, that's all. You are free to see in it what you like. That attic window will never be the symbol of misery; for that, it would have to be a sign, whereas it is a thing. The bad painter looks for the type. He paints the Arab, the Child, the Woman; the good one knows that neither the Arab nor the proletarian exists either in reality or on his canvas. He offers a workman, a certain workman. And what are we to think about a workman? An infinity of contradictory things. All thoughts and all feelings are there, adhering to the canvas in a state of profound undifferentiation. It is up to you to choose. Sometimes, high-minded artists try to move us. They paint long lines of workmen waiting in the snow to be hired, the emaciated faces of the unemployed, battlefields. They affect us no more than does Greuze with his "Prodigal Son." And that masterpiece, "The Massacre of Guernica," does any one think that it won over a single heart to the Spanish cause? And yet something is said that can never quite be heard and that would take an infinity of words to express. And Picasso's long harlequins, ambiguous and eternal, haunted with inexplicable meaning, inseparable from their stooping leanness and their pale diamond-shaped tights, are emotion become flesh, emotion which the flesh has absorbed as the blotter absorbs ink, and emotion which is unrecognizable, lost, strange to itself, scattered to the four corners of space and yet present to itself.

I have no doubt that charity or anger can produce other objects, but they will likewise be swallowed up; they will lose their name; there will remain only things haunted by a mysterious soul. One does not paint significations; one does not put them to music. Under these conditions, who would dare require that the painter or musician engage himself?

On the other hand, the writer deals with significations. Still, a distinction must be made. The empire of signs is prose; poetry is on the side of painting, sculpture, and music. I am accused of detesting it; the proof, so they say, is that *Les Temps Modernes* publishes very few poems. On the contrary, this is proof that we like it. To be convinced, all one need do is take a look at contemporary production. "At least," critics say triumphantly, "you can't even dream of engaging it." Indeed. But why should I want to? Because it uses words as does prose? But it does not use them in the same way, and it does not even *use* them at all. I should rather say that it serves them. Poets are men who refuse to *utilize* language. Now, since the quest for truth takes place in and by language conceived as a certain kind of instrument, it is unnecessary to imagine that they aim to discern or expound the true. Nor do they dream of *naming* the world, and, this being the case, they name nothing at all, for naming implies a perpetual sacrifice of the name to the object named, or, as Hegel would say, the name is revealed as the inessential in the face of the thing which is essential. They do not speak, neither do they keep still; it is something different. It has been said that they wanted to destroy the "word" by monstrous couplings, but this is false. For then they would have to be thrown into the midst of utilitarian language and would have had to try to retrieve words from it in odd little groups, as for example "horse" and "butter" by writing "horses of butter."[3]

Besides the fact that such an enterprise would require infinite time, it is not conceivable that one can keep oneself on the plane of the utilitarian project, consider words as instruments, and at the same contemplate taking their instrumentality away from them. In fact, the poet has withdrawn from language-instrument in a single movement. Once and for all he has chosen the poetic attitude which considers words as things and not as signs. For the ambiguity of the sign implies that one can penetrate it at

12

will like a pane of glass and pursue the thing signified, or turn his gaze toward its *reality* and consider it as an object. The man who talks is beyond words and near the object, whereas the poet is on this side of them. For the former, they are domesticated; for the latter they are in the wild state. For the former, they are useful conventions, tools which gradually wear out and which one throws away when they are no longer serviceable; for the latter, they are natural things which sprout naturally upon the earth like grass and trees.

But if he dwells upon words, as does the painter with colors and the musician with sounds, that does not mean that they have lost all signification in his eyes. Indeed, it is signification alone which can give words their verbal unity. Without it they are frittered away into sounds and strokes of the pen. Only, it too becomes natural. It is no longer the goal which is always out of reach and which human transcendence is always aiming at, but a property of each term, analogous to the expression of a face, to the little sad or gay meaning of sounds and colors. Having flowed into the word, having been absorbed by its sonority or visual aspect, having been thickened and defaced, it too is a thing, increate and eternal.

For the poet, language is a structure of the external world. The speaker is *in a situation* in language; he is invested with words. They are prolongations of his meanings, his pincers, his antennae, his eyeglasses. He maneuvers them from within; he feels them as if they were his body; he is surrounded by a verbal body which he is hardly aware of and which extends his action upon the world. The poet is outside of language. He sees words inside out as if he did not share the human condition, and as if he were first meeting the word as a barrier as he comes toward men. Instead of first knowing things by their name, it seems that first he has a silent contact with them, since, turning toward that other species of thing which for him is the word, touching them, testing them, palping them, he discovers in them a slight luminosity of their own and particular affinities with the earth, the sky, the water, and all created things.

Not knowing how to use them as a *sign* of an aspect of the world, he sees in the word the *image* of one of these aspects. And the verbal image he chooses for its resemblance to the willow tree or the ash tree is not necessarily the word which we use to designate these objects. As he is already on the outside, he considers words as a trap to catch a fleeing reality rather than as indicators which throw him out of himself into the midst of things. In short, all language is for him the mirror of the world. As a result, important changes take place in the internal economy of the word. Its sonority, its length, its masculine or feminine endings, its visual aspect, compose for him a face of flesh which *represents* rather than expresses signification. Inversely, as the signification is *realized*, the physical aspect of the word is reflected within it, and it, in its turn, functions as an image of the verbal body. Like its sign, too, for it has lost its pre-eminence; since words, like things, are increate, the poet does not decide whether the former exist for the latter or vice-versa.

Thus, between the word and the thing signified, there is established a double reciprocal relation of magical resemblance and signification. And the poet does not *utilize* the word, he does not choose between diverse acceptations; each of them, instead of appearing to him as an autonomous function, is given to him as a material quality which merges before his eyes with the other acceptation.

Thus, in each word he realizes, solely by the effect of the poetic *attitude*, the metaphors which Picasso dreamed of when he wanted to do a matchbox which was completely a bat without ceasing to be a matchbox. Florence is city, flower, and woman. It is city-flower, city-woman, and girl-flower all at the same time. And the strange object which thus appears has the liquidity of the *river*, the soft, tawny ardency of *gold*, and finally abandons itself with *propriety* and, by the continuous diminution of the silent *e*, prolongs indefinitely its modest blossoming.* To that is added the insidious effect of biography. For me, Florence is also a certain woman, an American actress who played in the silent films of my childhood, and about whom I have forgotten everything except that she was as long as a long evening glove and always a bit weary and always chaste and always married and misunderstood and whom I loved and whose name was Florence.

For the word, which tears the writer of prose away from himself and throws him into the midst of the world, sends back to the poet his own image, like a mirror.

---

*This sentence is not fully intelligible in translation as the author is here associating the component sounds of the word Florence with the signification of the French words they evoke. Thus: FL-OR-ENCE, *fleuve* (river), *or* (gold), and *décence* (propriety). The latter part of the sentence refers to the practice in French poetry of giving, in certain circumstances, a syllabic value to the otherwise silent terminal *e*.—Translator's note.

This is what justifies the double undertaking of Leiris who, on the one hand, in his *Glossary*, tries to give certain words a *poetic definition*, that is, one which is by itself a synthesis of reciprocal implications between the sonorous body and the verbal soul, and, on the other hand, in a still unpublished work, goes in quest of remembrance of things past, taking as guides a few words which for him are particularly charged with affectivity. Thus, the poetic word is a microcosm.

The crisis of language which broke out at the beginning of this century is a poetic crisis. Whatever the social and historical factors, it manifested itself by attacks of depersonalization of the writer in the face of words. He no longer knew how to use them, and, in Bergson's famous formula, he only half recognized them. He approached them with a completely fruitful feeling of strangeness. They were no longer his; they were no longer he; but in those strange mirrors, the sky, the earth, and his own life were reflected. And, finally, they became things themselves, or rather the black heart of things. And when the poet joins several of these microcosms together the case is like that of painters when they assemble their colors on the canvas. One might think that he is composing a sentence, but this is only what it appears to be. He is creating an object. The words-things are grouped by magical associations of fitness and incongruity, like colors and sounds. They attract, repel, and *"burn"* one another, and their association composes the veritable poetic unity which is the *phrase-object*.

More often the poet first has the scheme of the sentence in his mind, and the words follow. But this scheme has nothing in common with what one ordinarily calls a verbal scheme. It does not govern the construction of a signification. Rather, it is comparable to the creative project by which Picasso, even before touching his brush, prefigures in space the *thing* which will become a buffoon or a harlequin.

*To flee, to flee there, I feel that birds are drunk*
*But, oh, my heart, hear the song of the sailors.*
*(Fuir, là-bas fuir, je sens que des oiseaux sont ivres*
*Mais ô mon coeur entends le chant des matelots.)*

This "but" which rises like a monolith at the threshold of the sentence does not tie the second verse to the preceding one. It colors it with a certain reserved nuance, with "private associations" which penetrate it completely. In the same way, certain poems begin with "and." This conjunction no longer indicates to the mind an operation which is to be carried out; it extends throughout the paragraph to give it the absolute quality of a *sequel*. For the poet, the sentence has a tonality, a taste; by means of it he tastes for their own sake the irritating flavors of objection, of reserve, of disjunction. He carries them to the absolute. He makes them real properties of the sentence, which becomes an utter objection without being an objection *to* anything precise. He finds here those relations of reciprocal implication which we pointed out a short time ago between the poetic word and its meaning; the ensemble of the words chosen functions as an *image* of the interrogative or restrictive nuance, and vice-

17

versa, the interrogation is an image of the verbal ensemble which it delimits.

As in the following admirable verses:

> *Oh seasons! Oh castles!*
> *What soul is faultless?*
> *(O saisons! O châteaux!*
> *Quelle âme est sans défaut?)*

Nobody is questioned; nobody is questioning; the poet is absent. And the question involves no answer, or rather it is its own answer. Is it therefore a false question? But it would be absurd to believe that Rimbaud "meant" that everybody has his faults. As Breton said of Saint-Pol Roux, "If he had meant it, he would have said it." Nor did he *mean* to say something else. He asked an absolute question. He conferred upon the beautiful word "soul" an interrogative existence. The interrogation has become a thing as the anguish of Tintoretto became a yellow sky. It is no longer a signification, but a substance. It is seen from the outside, and Rimbaud invites us to see it from the outside with him. Its strangeness arises from the fact that, in order to consider it, we place ourselves on the other side of the human condition, on the side of God.

If this is the case, one easily understands how foolish it would be to require a poetic engagement. Doubtless, emotion, even passion — and why not anger, social indignation, and political hatred? — are at the origin of the poem. But they are not *expressed* there, as in a pamphlet or in a confession. Insofar as the writer of prose exhibits feelings, he illustrates them; whereas, if the poet injects his feelings into his poem, he ceases to recognize them; the words take hold of them, penetrate them, and metamorphose them; they do not signify them, even in his eyes. Emotion has become thing; it now has the opacity of things; it is compounded by the ambiguous properties of the vocables in which it has been enclosed. And above all, there is always much more in each phrase, in each verse, as there is more than simple anguish in the yellow sky over Golgotha. The word, the phrase-thing, inexhaustible as things, everywhere overflows the feeling which has produced them. How can one hope to provoke the indignation or the political enthusiasm of the reader when the very thing one does is to withdraw him from the human condition and invite him to consider with the eyes of God a language that has been turned inside out? Someone may say, "You're forgetting the poets of the Resistance. You're forgetting Pierre Emmanuel." Not a bit! They're the very ones I was going to give as examples.[4]

But even if the poet is forbidden to engage himself, is that a reason for exempting the writer of prose? What do they have in common? It is true that the prosewriter and the poet both write. But there is nothing in common between these two acts of writing except the movement of the hand which traces the letters. Otherwise, their universes are incommunicable, and what is good for one is not good for the other. Prose is, in essence, utilitarian. I would readily define the prose-writer as a man who *makes use* of words. M. Jourdan made prose to ask for his slippers, and Hitler to declare war on Poland. The writer is a *speaker*; he designates, demonstrates, orders, refuses, interpolates, begs, insults, persuades, insinuates. If he does so without any effect, he does not therefore become a poet; he is a writer who is talking and saying nothing. We have seen enough of language inside out; it is now time to look at it right side out.[5]

The art of prose is employed in discourse; its substance is by nature significative; that is, the words are first of all not objects but designations for objects; it is not first of all a matter of knowing whether they please or displease in themselves, but whether they correctly indicate a certain thing or a certain notion. Thus, it often happens that we find ourselves possessing a certain idea that someone has taught us by means of words without being able to recall a single one of the words which have transmitted it to us.

Prose is first of all an attitude of mind. As Valéry would say, there is prose when the word passes across our gaze as the glass across the sun. When one is in danger or in difficulty he grabs any instrument. When the danger is past, he does not even remember whether it was a hammer or a stick; moreover, he never knew; all he needed was a prolongation of his body, a means of extending his hand to the highest branch. It was a sixth finger, a third leg, in short, a pure function which he assimilated. Thus, regarding language, it is our shell and our antennae; it protects us against others and informs us about them; it is a prolongation of our senses, a third eye which is going to look into our neighbor's heart. We are within language as within our body. We *feel* it spontaneously while going beyond it toward other ends, as we feel our hands and our feet; we perceive it when it is the other who is using it, as we perceive the limbs of

20

others. There is the word which is lived and the word which is met. But in both cases it is in the course of an undertaking, either of me acting upon others, or the other upon me. The word is a certain particular moment of action and has no meaning outside of it. In certain cases of aphasia the possibilities of acting, of understanding situations, and of having normal relations with the other sex, are lost.

At the heart of this apraxia the destruction of language appears only as the collapse of one of the structures, the finest and the most apparent. And if prose is never anything but the privileged instrument of a certain undertaking, if it is only the poet's business to contemplate words in a disinterested fashion, then one has the right to ask the prose-writer from the very start, "What is your aim in writing? What undertakings are you engaged in, and why does it require you to have recourse to writing?" In any case this undertaking cannot have pure contemplation as an end. For, intuition is silence, and the end of language is to communicate. One can doubtless *pin down* the results of intuition, but in this case a few words hastily scrawled on paper will suffice; it will always be enough for the author to recognize what he had in mind. If the words are assembled into sentences, with a concern for clarity, a decision foreign to the intuition, to the language itself, must intervene, the decision of confiding to others the results obtained. In each case one must ask the reason for this decision. And the common sense which our pedants too readily forget never stops repeating it. Are we not in the habit of putting this basic question to young people who are thinking of writing: "Do you have anything to say?" Which means: something which is worth the trouble of being communicated. But what do we mean by something which is "worth the trouble" if it is not by recourse to a system of transcendent values?

Moreover, to consider only this secondary structure of the undertaking, which is what the *verbal moment* is, the serious error of pure stylists is to think that the word is a gentle breeze which plays lightly over the surface of things, which grazes them without altering them, and that the speaker is a pure *witness* who sums up with a word his harmless contemplation. To speak is to act; anything which one names is already no longer quite the same; it has lost its innocence.

If you name the behavior of an individual, you reveal it to him; he sees himself. And since you are at the same time naming it to all others, he knows that he is *seen* at the moment he *sees* himself. The furtive gesture which he forgot while making it, begins to exist beyond all measure, to exist for everybody; it is integrated into the objective mind; it takes on new dimensions; it is retrieved. After that, how can you expect him to act in the same way? Either he will persist in his behavior out of obstinacy and with full knowledge of what he is doing, or he will give it up. Thus, by speaking, I reveal the situation by my very intention of changing it; I reveal it to myself and to others *in order* to change it. I strike at its very heart, I transpierce it, and I display it in full view; at present I dispose of it; with every word I utter, I involve myself a little more in the world, and by the same token

22

I emerge from it a little more, since I go beyond it toward the future.

Thus, the prose-writer is a man who has chosen a certain method of secondary action which we may call action by disclosure. It is therefore permissible to ask him this second question: "What aspect of the world do you want to disclose? What change do you want to bring into the world by this disclosure?" The "engaged" writer knows that words are action. He knows that to reveal is to change and that one can reveal only by planning to change. He has given up the impossible dream of giving an impartial picture of Society and the human condition. Man is the being toward whom no being can be impartial, not even God. For God, if He existed, would be, as certain mystics have seen Him, in a *situation* in relationship to man. And He is also the being Who can not even see a situation without changing it, for His gaze congeals, destroys, or sculpts, or, as does eternity, changes the object in itself. It is in love, in hate, in anger, in fear, in joy, in indignation, in admiration, in hope, in despair, that man and the world reveal themselves *in their truth.* Doubtless, the engaged writer can be mediocre; he can even be conscious of being so; but as one can not write without the intention of succeeding perfectly, the modesty with which he envisages his work should not divert him from constructing it *as if* it were to have the greatest celebrity. He should never say to himself "Bah! I'll be lucky if I have three thousand readers," but rather, "What would happen if everybody read what I wrote?" He remembers what Mosca said beside the coach which carried Fabrizio and Sanseverina away, "If the word Love

23

comes up between them, I'm lost." He knows that he is the man who names what has not yet been named or what dares not tell its name. He knows that he makes the word "love" and the word "hate" *surge up* and with them love and hate between men who had not yet decided upon their feelings. He knows that words, as Brice-Parrain says, are "loaded pistols." If he speaks, he fires. He may be silent, but since he has chosen to fire, he must do it like a man, by aiming at targets, and not like a child, at random, by shutting his eyes and firing merely for the pleasure of hearing the shot go off.

Later on we shall try to determine what the goal of literature may be. But from this point on we may conclude that the writer has chosen to reveal the world and particularly to reveal man to other men so that the latter may assume full responsibility before the object which has been thus laid bare. It is assumed that no one is ignorant of the law because there is a code and because the law is written down; thereafter, you are free to violate it, but you know the risks you run. Similarly, the function of the writer is to act in such a way that nobody can be ignorant of the world and that nobody may say that he is innocent of what it's all about. And since he has once engaged himself in the universe of language, he can never again pretend that he can not speak. Once you enter the universe of significations, there is nothing you can do to get out of it. Let words organize themselves freely and they will make sentences, and each sentence contains language in its entirety and refers back to the whole universe. Silence itself is defined in relationship to words, as the pause in music receives its meaning from the group of notes around it. This silence is a moment of language; being silent is not being dumb; it is to refuse to speak, and therefore to keep on speaking. Thus, if a writer has chosen to remain silent on any aspect whatever of the world, or, according to an expression which says just what it means, to *pass over* it in silence, one has the right to ask him a third question: "Why have you spoken of this rather than that, and—since you speak in order to bring about change—why do you want to change this rather than that?"

All this does not prevent there being a manner of writing. One is not a writer for having chosen to say certain things, but for having chosen to say them in a certain way. And, to be sure, the style makes the value of the prose. But it should pass unnoticed. Since words are transparent and since the gaze looks through them, it would be absurd to slip in among them some panes of rough glass. Beauty is in this case only a gentle and imperceptible force. In a painting it shines forth at the very first sight; in a book it hides itself; it acts by persuasion like the charm of a voice or a face. It does not coerce; it inclines a person without his suspecting it, and he thinks that he is yielding to arguments when he is really being solicited by a charm that he does not see. The ceremonial of the mass is not faith; it disposes the harmony of words; their beauty, the balance of the phrases, *dispose* the passions of the reader without his being aware and orders them like the mass, like music, like the dance. If he happens to consider them by themselves, he loses the meaning; there remains only a boring seesaw of phrases.

In prose the aesthetic pleasure is pure only if it is

thrown into the bargain. I blush at recalling such simple ideas, but it seems that today they have been forgotten. If that were not the case, would we be told that we are planning the murder of literature, or, more simply, that engagement is harmful to the art of writing? If the contamination of a certain kind of prose by poetry had not confused the ideas of our critics, would they dream of attacking us on the matter of form, when we have never spoken of anything but the content? There is nothing to be said about form in advance, and we have said nothing. Everyone invents his own, and one judges it afterward. It is true that the subjects suggest the style, but they do not order it. There are no styles ranged a priori outside of the literary art. What is more engaged, what is more boring than the idea of attacking the Jesuits? Yet, out of this Pascal made his *Provincial Letters*. In short, it is a matter of knowing what one wants to write about, whether butterflies or the condition of the Jews. And when one knows, then it remains to decide how one will write about it.

Often the two choices are only one, but among good writers the second choice never precedes the first. I know that Giraudoux has said that "the only concern is finding the style; the idea comes afterwards;" but he was wrong. The idea did not come. On the contrary, if one considers subjects as problems which are always open, as solicitations, as expectations, it will be easily understood that art loses nothing in engagement. On the contrary, just as physics submits to mathematicians new problems which require them to produce a new symbolism, in like manner the always new requirements of the social and the metaphysical engage the artist in finding a new language and new techniques. If we no longer write as they did in the eighteenth century, it is because the language of Racine and Saint-Evremond does not lend itself to talking about locomotives or the proletariat. After that, the purists will perhaps forbid us to write about locomotives. But art has never been on the side of the purists.

If that is the principle of engagement, what objection can one have to it? And above all *what objection has been made to it?* It has seemed to me that my opponents have not had their hearts in their work very much and that their articles contain nothing more than a long scandalized sigh which drags on over two or three columns. I should have liked to know *in the name of what,* with what conception of literature, they condemned engagement. But they have not said; they themselves have not known. The most reasonable thing would have been to support their condemnation on the old theory of art for art's sake. But none of them can accept it. That is also disturbing. We know very well that pure art and empty art are the same thing and that aesthetic purism was a brilliant maneuver of the bourgeois of the last century who preferred to see themselves denounced as philistines rather than as exploiters. Therefore, they themselves admitted that the writer had to speak about something. But about what? I believe that their embarrassment would have been extreme if Fernandez had not found for them, after the other war, the notion of the *message.* The writer of today, they say, should in no case occupy himself with temporal affairs. Neither should he set up lines without signification nor seek solely beauty of phrase and of imagery. His function is to deliver messages to his readers. Well, what is a message?

It must be borne in mind that most critics are men who have not had much luck and who, just about the time they were growing desperate, found a quiet little job as cemetery watchmen. God knows whether cemeteries are peaceful; none of them are more cheerful than a library. The dead are there; the only thing they have done is write. They have long since been washed clean of the sin of living, and besides, their lives are known only through other books which other dead men have written about them. Rimbaud is dead. So are Paterne Berrichon and Isabelle Rimbaud. The trouble makers have disappeared; all that remains are the little coffins that are stacked on shelves along the walls like urns in a columbarium. The critic lives badly; his wife does not appreciate him as she ought to; his children are ungrateful; the first of the month is hard on him. But it is always possible for him to enter his library, take down a book from the shelf, and open it. It gives off a slight odor of the cellar, and a strange operation begins which he has decided to call reading. From one point of view it is a possession; he lends his body to the dead in order that they may come back to life. And from another point of view it is a contact with the beyond. Indeed, the book is by no means an object; neither is it an act, nor even a thought. Written by a dead man about dead things, it no longer has any place on this earth; it speaks of nothing which interests us directly. Left to itself, it falls back and collapses; there remain only ink spots on musty paper. And when the critic reanimates these spots, when he makes letters and words of them, they speak to him of passions which he does not feel, of bursts of anger without objects, of dead fears and hopes. It is a whole disembodied world which surrounds him, where human feelings, because they are no longer affecting, have passed on to the status of exemplary feelings and, in a word, of *values*. So he persuades himself that he has entered into relations with an intelligible world which is like the truth of his daily sufferings. And their reason for being. He thinks that nature imitates art, as for Plato the world of the senses imitates that of the archetypes. And during the time he is reading, his everyday life becomes an appearance. His nagging wife, his hunchbacked son, they too are appearances. And he will put up with them because Xenophon has drawn the portrait of Xantippe and Shakespeare that of Richard the Third.

It is a holiday for him when contemporary authors do him the favor of dying. Their books, too raw, too living, too urgent, pass on to the other shore; they become less and less affecting and more and more beautiful. After a short stay in Purgatory they go on to people the intelligible heaven with new values. Bergotte, Swann, Siegfried and Bella, and Monsieur Teste are recent acquisitions. He is waiting for Nathanaël and Ménalque. As for the writers who persist in living, he asks them only not to move about too much, and to make an effort to resemble from now on the dead men they will be. Valéry, who for twenty-five years had been publishing posthumous books, managed the matter very nicely. That is why, like some highly exceptional saints, he was canonized during his lifetime. But Malraux is scandalous.

Our critics are Catharians. They don't want to have anything to do with the real world except eat and drink in it, and since it is absolutely necessary to have relations with our fellow-creatures, they have chosen to have them with the defunct. They get excited only about classified matters, closed quarrels, stories whose ends are known. They never bet on uncertain issues, and since history has decided for them, since the objects which terrified or angered the authors they read have disappeared, since bloody disputes seem futile at a distance of two centuries, they can be charmed with balanced periods, and everything happens for them as if all literature were only a vast tautology and as if every new prose-writer had invented a new way of speaking only for the purpose of saying nothing.

To speak of archetypes and "human nature" — is that speaking in order to say nothing? All the conceptions of our critics oscillate from one idea to the other. And, of course, both of them are false. Our great writers wanted to destroy, to edify, to demonstrate. But we no longer retain the proofs which they have advanced because we have no concern with what they mean to prove. The abuses which they denounced are no longer those of our time. There are others which rouse us which they did not suspect. History has given the lie to some of their predictions, and those which have been fulfilled became true so long ago that we have forgotten that they were at first flashes of their genius. Some of their thoughts are utterly dead, and there are others which the whole human race has taken up to its advantage and which we now regard as commonplace. It follows that the best arguments of these writers have lost their effectiveness. We admire only their order and rigor. Their most compact composition is in our eyes only an ornament, an elegant architecture of exposition, with no more practical application than such architectures as the fugues of Bach and the arabesques of the Alhambra.

We are still moved by the passion of these impassioned geometries when the geometry no longer convinces us. Or rather by the representation of the passion. In the course of centuries the ideas have turned flat, but they remain the little personal objectives of a man who was once flesh and bone; behind the reasons of reason, which languish, we perceive the reasons of the heart, the virtues, the vices, and that great pain that men have in living. Sade does his best to win us over, but we hardly find him scandalous. He is no longer anything but a soul eaten by a beautiful disease, a pearl-oyster. The *Letter on the Theater* no longer keeps anyone from going to the theater, but we find it piquant that Rousseau detested the art of the drama. If we are a bit versed in psychoanalysis, our pleasure is perfect. We shall explain the *Social Contract* by the Oedipus complex and *The Spirit of the Laws* by the inferiority complex. That is, we shall fully enjoy the well-known superiority of live dogs to dead lions. Thus, when a book presents befuddled thoughts which appear to be reasons only to melt under scrutiny and to be reduced to heart beats, when the teaching that one can draw from it is radically different from what its author intended, the book is called a message. Rousseau,

31

the father of the French Revolution, and Gobineau, the father of racism, both sent us messages. And the critic considers them with equal sympathy. If they were alive, he would have to choose between the two, to love one and hate the other. But what brings them together, above all, is that they are both profoundly and deliciously wrong, and in the same way: they are dead.

Thus, contemporary writers should be advised to deliver messages, that is, voluntarily to limit their writing to the involuntary expression of their souls. I say involuntary because the dead, from Montaigne to Rimbaud, have painted themselves completely, but without having meant to — it is something they have simply thrown into the bargain. The surplus which they have given us unintentionally should be the primary and professed goal of living writers. They are not to be forced to give us confessions without any dressing, nor are they to abandon themselves to the too-naked lyricism of the romantics. But since we find pleasure in foiling the ruses of Chateaubriand or Rousseau, in surprising them in the secret places of their being at the moment they are playing at being the public man, in distinguishing the private motives from their most universal assertions, we shall ask newcomers to procure us this pleasure deliberately. So let them reason, assert, deny, refute, and prove; but the cause they are defending must be only the apparent aim of their discourse; the deeper goal is to yield themselves without seeming to do so. They must first disarm themselves of their arguments as time has done for those of the classic writers; they must bring them to bear upon subjects which interest no one or on truths so general that readers are convinced in advance. As for their ideas, they must give them an air of profundity, but with an effect of emptiness, and they must shape them in such a way that they are obviously explained by an unhappy childhood, a class hatred, or an incestuous love. Let them not presume to think in earnest; thought conceals the man, and it is the man alone who interests us. A bare tear is not lovely. It offends. A good argument also offends, as Stendhal well observed. But an argument that masks a tear — that's what we're after. The argument removes the obscenity from the tears; the tears, by revealing their origin in the passions, remove the aggressiveness from the argument. We shall be neither too deeply touched nor at all convinced, and we shall be able to yield ourselves in security to that moderate pleasure which, as everyone knows, we derive from the contemplation of works of art. Thus, this is "true," "pure" literature, a subjectivity which yields itself under the aspect of the objective, a discourse so curiously contrived that it is equivalent to silence, a thought which debates with itself, a reason which is only the mask of madness, an Eternal which lets it be understood that it is only a moment of History, a historical moment which, by the hidden side which it reveals, suddenly sends back a perpetual lesson to the eternal man, but which is produced against the express wishes of those who do the teaching.

When all is said and done, the message is a soul which is made object. A soul, and what is to be done with a soul? One contemplates it at a respectful distance. It is not customary to show one's soul in society without an imperious motive. But, with certain reserves, convention permits some individuals to put theirs into commerce, and all adults may procure it for themselves. For many people today, works of the mind are thus little straying souls which one acquires at a modest price; there is good old Montaigne's, dear La Fontaine's, and that of Jean-Jacques and of Jean-Paul and of delicious Gérard. What is called literary art is the ensemble of the treatments which make them inoffensive. Tanned, refined, chemically treated, they provide their acquirers with the opportunity of devoting some moments of a life completely turned outward to the cultivation of subjectivity. Custom guarantees it to be without risk. Montaigne's skepticism? Who can take it seriously since the author of the *Essays* got frightened when the plague ravaged Bordeaux? Or Rousseau's humanitarianism, since "Jean-Jacques" put his children into an orphanage? And the strange revelations of *Sylvie,* since Gérard de Nerval was mad? At the very most, the professional critic will set up infernal dialogues between them and will inform us that French thought is a perpetual colloquy between Pascal and Montaigne. In so doing he has no intention of making Pascal and Montaigne more alive, but of making Malraux and Gide more dead. Finally, when the internal contradictions of the life and the work have made both of them useless, when the message, in its imponderable depth, has taught us these capital truths, "that man is neither good nor bad," "that there is a great deal of suffering in human life," "that genius is only great patience," this melancholy cuisine will have achieved its purpose, and the reader, as he lays down the book, will be able to cry out with a tranquil soul, "All this is only literature."

34

But since, for us, writing is an enterprise; since writers are alive before being dead; since we think that we must try to be as right as we can in our books; and since, even if the centuries show us to be in the wrong, this is no reason to show in advance that we are wrong; since we think that the writer should engage himself completely in his works, and not as an abject passivity by putting forward his vices, his misfortunes, and his weaknesses, but as a resolute will and as a choice, as this total enterprise of living that each one of us is, it is then proper that we take up this problem at its beginning and that we, in our turn, ask ourselves: *"Why* does one write?"

## NOTES

1. At least in general. The greatness and error of Klee lie in his attempt to make a painting both sign and object.

2. I say "create," not "imitate," which is enough to squelch the bombast of M. Charles Estienne who has obviously not understood a word of my argument and who is dead set on tilting at shadows.

3. This is the example cited by Bataille in *Inner Experience*.

4. If one wishes to know the origin of this attitude toward language, the following are a few brief indications.

Originally, poetry creates the *myth*, while the prose-writer draws its *portrait*. In reality, the human act, governed by needs and urged on by the useful is, in a sense, a *means*. It passes unnoticed, and it is the result which counts. When I extend my hand *in order to* take up my pen, I have only a fleeting and obscure consciousness of my gesture; it is the pen which I see. Thus, man is alienated by his ends. Poetry reverses the relationship: the world and things become inessential, become a pretext for the act which becomes its own end. The vase is there so that the girl may perform the graceful act of filling it; the Trojan War, so that Hector and Achilles may engage in that heroic combat. The action, detached from its goals, which become blurred, becomes an act of prowess or a dance. Nevertheless, however indifferent he might have been to the success of the enterprise, the poet, before the nineteenth century, remained in harmony with society as a whole. He did not use language for the end which prose seeks, but he had the same confidence in it as the prose-writer.

With the coming of bourgeois society, the poet puts up a common front with the prose-writer to declare it unlivable. His job is always to create the myth of man, but he passes from white magic to black magic. Man is always presented as the absolute end, but by the success of his enterprise he is sucked into a utilitarian collectivity. The thing that is in the background of his act and that will allow transition to the myth is thus no longer success, but defeat. By stopping the infinite series of his projects like a screen, defeat alone returns him to himself in his purity. The world remains the inessential, but it is now there as a pretext for defeat. The finality of the thing is to send man back to himself by blocking the route. Moreover, it is not a matter of arbitrarily introducing defeat and ruin into the course of the world, but rather of having no eyes for anything but that. Human enterprise has two aspects: it is both success and failure. The dialectical scheme is inadequate for reflecting upon it. We must make our vocabulary and the frames of our reason more supple. Some day I am going to try to describe that strange reality, History, which is neither objective, nor ever quite subjective, in which the dialectic is contested, penetrated, and corroded by a kind of antidialectic, but which is still a dialectic. But that is the philosopher's affair. One does not ordinarily consider the two faces of Janus; the man of action sees one and the poet sees the other. When the instruments are broken and unusable, when plans are blasted and effort is useless, the world appears with a childlike and terrible freshness, without supports, without paths. It has the maximum reality because it is crushing for man, and as action, in any case, generalizes, defeat restores to things their individual reality. But, by an expected reversal, the defeat, considered as a final end, is both a contesting and an appropriation of this universe. A contesting, because man *is worth more* than that which crushes; he no longer contests things in their "little bit of reality," like the engineer or the captain, but, on the contrary, in their "too full of reality," by his very existence as a vanquished person; he is the remorse of the world. An appropriation, because the world, by ceasing to be the tool of success, becomes the instrument of failure. So there it is, traversed by an obscure finality; it is its coefficient of adversity which serves, the more human insofar as it is more hostile to man. The defeat itself turns into salvation. Not that it makes us yield to some "beyond," but by itself it shifts and is metamorphosed. For example, poetic language rises out of the ruins of prose. If it is true that the word is a betrayal and that communication is impossible, then each word by itself recovers its individuality and becomes an instrument of our defeat and a receiver of the incommunicable. It is not that there is *another thing* to communicate; but the communication of prose having miscarried, it is the very meaning of the word which becomes the pure incommunicable. Thus, the failure of communication becomes a suggestion of the incommunicable, and the thwarted project of utilizing words is succeeded by the pure disinterested intuition of the word. Thus, we again meet with the description which we attempted earlier in this study, but in the more general perspective of the absolute valorization of the defeat, which seems to me the original attitude of contemporary poetry. Note also that this choice confers upon the poet a very precise function in the collectivity: in a highly integrated or religious society, the defeat is masked by the State or redeemed by Religion; in a less integrated and secular society, such as our democracies, it is up to poetry to redeem them.

Poetry is a case of the loser winning. And the genuine poet chooses to lose, even if he has to go so far as to die, in order to win. I repeat that I am talking of contemporary poetry. History presents other forms of poetry. It is not my concern to show their connection with ours. Thus, if one absolutely wishes to speak of the engagement of the poet, let us say that he is the man who engages himself to lose. This is the deeper meaning of that tough-luck, of that malediction with which he always claims kinship and which he always attributes to an intervention from without; whereas it is his deepest choice, the source, and not the consequence of his poetry. He is certain of the total defeat of the human enterprise and arranges to fail in his own life in order to bear witness, by his individual defeat, to human defeat in general. Thus, he contests, as we shall see, which is what the prose-writer does too. But the contesting of prose is carried on in the name of a greater success; and that of poetry, in the name of the hidden defeat which every victory conceals.

5. It goes without saying that in all poetry a certain form of prose, that is, of success, is present; and, vice-versa, the driest prose always contains a bit of poetry, that is, a certain form of defeat; no prose-writer is *quite* capable of expressing what he wants to say; he says too much or not enough; each phrase is a wager, a risk assumed; the more cautious one is, the more attention the word attracts; as Valéry has shown, no one can understand a word to its very bottom. Thus, each word is used simultaneously for its clear and social meaning and for certain obscure resonances — let me say, almost for its physiognomy. The reader, too, is sensitive to this. At once we are no longer on the level of concerted communication, but on that of grace and chance; the silences of prose are poetic because they mark its limits, and it is for the purpose of greater clarity that I have been considering the extreme cases of pure prose and pure poetry. However, it need not be concluded that we can pass from poetry to prose by a continuous series of intermediate forms. If the prose-writer is too eager to fondle his words, the *eidos* of "prose" is shattered and we fall into highfalutin nonsense. If the poet relates, explains, or teaches, the poetry becomes *prosaic*; he has lost the game. It is a matter of complex structures, impure, but well-defined.

## II

## WHY WRITE?

Each one has his reasons: for one, art is a flight; for another, a means of conquering. But one can flee into a hermitage, into madness, into death. One can conquer by arms. Why does it have to be *writing*, why does one have to manage his escapes and conquests by *writing*? Because, behind the various aims of authors, there is a deeper and more immediate choice which is common to all of us. We shall try to elucidate this choice, and we shall see whether it is not in the name of this very choice of writing that the engagement of writers must be required.

Each of our perceptions is accompanied by the consciousness that human reality is a "revealer," that is, it is through human reality that "there is" being, or, to put it differently, that man is the means by which things are manifested. It is our presence in the world which multiplies relations. It is we who set up a relationship between this tree and that bit of sky. Thanks to us, that star which has been dead for millennia, that quarter moon, and that dark river are disclosed in the unity of a landscape. It is the speed of our auto and our airplane which organizes the great masses of the earth. With each of our acts, the world reveals to us a new face. But, if we know that we are directors of being, we also know that we are not its producers. If we turn away from this landscape, it will sink back into its dark permanence. At least, it will sink back; there is no one mad enough to think that it is going to be annihilated. It is we who shall be annihilated, and the earth will remain in its lethargy until another consciousness comes along to awaken it. Thus, to our inner certainty of being "revealers" is added that of being inessential in relation to the thing revealed.

One of the chief motives of artistic creation is certainly the need of feeling that we are essential in relationship to the world. If I fix on canvas or in writing a certain aspect of the fields or the sea or a look on someone's face which I have disclosed, I am conscious of having produced them by condensing relationships, by introducing order where there was none, by imposing the unity of mind on the diversity of things. That is, I feel myself essential in relation to my creation. But this time it is the created object which escapes me; I can not reveal and produce at the same time. The creation becomes inessential in relation to the creative activity. First of all, even if it appears to others as definitive, the created object always seems to us in a state of suspension; we can always change this line, that shade, that word. Thus, it never *forces itself*. A novice painter asked his teacher, "When should I consider my painting finished?" And the teacher answered, "When you can look at it in amazement and say to yourself '*I'm* the one who did *that!*'"

Which amounts to saying "never." For it is virtually

39

considering one's work with someone else's eyes and revealing what one has created. But it is self-evident that we are proportionally less conscious of the thing produced and more conscious of our productive activity. When it is a matter of pottery or carpentry, we work according to traditional norms, with tools whose usage is codified; it is Heidegger's famous "they" who are working with our hands. In this case, the result can seem to us sufficiently strange to preserve its objectivity in our eyes. But if we ourselves produce the rules of production, the measures, the criteria, and if our creative drive comes from the very depths of our heart, then we never find anything but ourselves in our work. It is we who have invented the laws by which we judge it. It is our history, our love, our gaiety that we recognize in it. Even if we should regard it without touching it any further, we never *receive* from it that gaiety or love. We put them into it. The results which we have obtained on canvas or paper never seem to us *objective*. We are too familiar with the processes of which they are the effects. These processes remain a subjective discovery; they are ourselves, our inspiration, our ruse, and when we seek to *perceive* our work, we create it again, we repeat mentally the operations which produced it; each of its aspects appears as a result. Thus, in the perception, the object is given as the essential thing and the subject as the inessential. The latter seeks essentiality in the creation and obtains it, but then it is the object which becomes the inessential.

This dialectic is nowhere more apparent than in the art of writing, for the literary object is a peculiar top which exists only in movement. To make it come into view a concrete act called reading is necessary, and it lasts only as long as this act can last. Beyond that, there are only black marks on paper. Now, the writer can not read what he writes, whereas the shoemaker can put on the shoes he has just made if they are his size, and the architect can live in the house he has built. In reading, one foresees; one waits. He foresees the end of the sentence, the following sentence, the next page. He waits for them to confirm or disappoint his foresights. The reading is composed of a host of hypotheses, of dreams followed by awakenings, of hopes and deceptions. Readers are always ahead of the sentence they are reading in a merely probable future which partly collapses and partly comes together in proportion as they progress, which withdraws from one page to the next and forms the moving horizon of the literary object. Without waiting, without a future, without ignorance, there is no objectivity.

Now the operation of writing involves an implicit quasi-reading which makes real reading impossible. When the words form under his pen, the author doubtless sees them, but he does not see them as the reader does, since he knows them before writing them down. The function of his gaze is not to reveal, by stroking them, the sleeping words which are waiting to be read, but to control the sketching of the signs. In short, it is a purely regulating mission, and the view before him reveals nothing except for slight slips of the pen. The writer neither foresees nor conjectures; he *projects*. It often happens that he awaits, as they say, the inspiration. But one does not wait for himself the way he waits for others. If he hesitates, he knows that the future is not made, that he himself is going to make it, and if he still does not know what is going to happen to his hero, that simply means that he has not thought about it, that he has not decided upon anything. The future is then a blank page, whereas the future of the reader is two hundred pages filled with words which separate him from the end. Thus, the writer meets everywhere only *his* knowledge, *his* will, *his* plans, in short, himself. He touches only his own subjectivity; the object he creates is out of reach; he does not create it *for himself*. If he rereads himself, it is already too late. The sentence will never quite be a thing in his eyes. He goes to the very limits of the subjective but without crossing it. He appreciates the effect of a touch, of an epigram, of a well-placed adjective, but it is the effect they will have on others. He can judge it, not feel it. Proust never discovered the homosexuality of Charlus, since he had decided upon it even before starting on his book. And if a day comes when the book takes on for its author a semblance of objectivity, it is that years have passed, that he has forgotten it, that its spirit is quite foreign to him, and doubtless he is no longer capable of writing it. This was the case with Rousseau when he reread the *Social Contract* at the end of his life.

Thus, it is not true that one writes for himself. That would be the worst blow. In projecting his emotions on paper, one barely manages to give them a languishing extension. The creative act is only an incomplete and abstract moment in the production of a work. If the author existed alone he would be able to write as much as he liked; the work as *object* would never see the light of day and he would either have to put down his pen or despair. But the operation of writing implies that of reading as its dialectical correlative and these two connected acts necessitate two distinct agents. It is the conjoint effort of author and reader which brings upon the scene that concrete and imaginary object which is the work of the mind. There is no art except for and by others.

Reading seems, in fact, to be the synthesis of perception and creation.[1] It supposes the essentiality of both the subject and the object. The object is essential because it is strictly transcendent, because it imposes its own structures, and because one must wait for it and observe it; but the subject is also essential because it is required not only to disclose the object (that is, to make *there be* an object) but also so that this object might *be* (that is, to produce it). In a word, the reader is conscious of disclosing in creating, of creating by disclosing. In reality, it is not necessary to believe that reading is a mechanical operation and that signs make an impression upon him as light does on a photographic plate. If he is inattentive, tired, stupid, or thoughtless, most of the relations will escape him. He will never manage to "catch on" to the object (in the sense in which we see that fire "catches" or "doesn't catch"). He will draw some phrases out of the shadow, but they will seem to appear as random strokes. If he is at his best, he will project beyond the words a synthetic form, each phrase of which will be no more than a partial function: the "theme," the "subject," or the "meaning." Thus, from the very beginning, the

1. The same is true in different degrees regarding the spectator's attitude before other works of art (paintings, symphonies, statues, etc.)

meaning is no longer contained in the words, since it is he, on the contrary, who allows the signification of each of them to be understood; and the literary object, though realized *through* language, is never given *in* language. On the contrary, it is by nature a silence and an opponent of the word. In addition, the hundred thousand words aligned in a book can be read one by one so that the meaning of the work does not emerge. Nothing is accomplished if the reader does not put himself from the very beginning and almost without a guide at the height of this silence; if, in short, he does not invent it and does not then place there, and hold on to, the words and sentences which he awakens. And if I am told that it would be more fitting to call this operation a re-invention or a discovery, I shall answer that, first, such a re-invention would be as new and as original an act as the first invention. And, especially, when an object has never existed before, there can be no question of re-inventing it or discovering it. For if the silence about which I am speaking is really the goal at which the author is aiming, he has, at least, never been familiar with it; his silence is subjective and anterior to language. It is the absence of words, the undifferentiated and lived silence of inspiration, which the word will then particularize, whereas the silence produced by the reader is an object. And at the very interior of this object there are more silences—which the author does not tell. It is a question of silences which are so particular that they could not retain any meaning outside of the object which the reading causes to appear. However, it is these which give it its density and its particular face.

To say that they are unexpressed is hardly the word; for they are precisely the inexpressible. And that is why one does not come upon them at any definite moment in the reading; they are everywhere and nowhere. The quality of the marvelous in *The Wanderer* (*Le Grand Meaulnes*), the grandiosity of *Armance*, the degree of realism and truth of Kafka's mythology, these are never given. The reader must invent them all in a continual exceeding of the written thing. To be sure, the author guides him, but all he does is guide him. The landmarks he sets up are separated by the void. The reader must unite them; he must go beyond them. In short, reading is directed creation.

On the one hand, the literary object has no other substance than the reader's subjectivity; Raskolnikov's waiting is *my* waiting which I lend him. Without this impatience of the reader he would remain only a collection of signs. His hatred of the police magistrate who questions him is my hatred which has been solicited and wheedled out of me by signs, and the police magistrate himself would not exist without the hatred I have for him via Raskolnikov. That is what animates him, it is his very flesh.

But on the other hand, the words are there like traps to arouse our feelings and to reflect them toward us. Each word is a path of transcendence; it shapes our feelings, names them, and attributes them to an imaginary personage who takes it upon himself to live them for us and who has no other substance than these borrowed passions; he confers objects, perspectives, and a horizon upon them.

Thus, for the reader, all is to do and all is already done; the work exists only at the exact level of his capacities; while he reads and creates, he knows that he can always go further in his reading, can always create more profoundly, and thus the work seems to him as inexhaustible and opaque as things. We would readily reconcile that "rational intuition" which Kant reserved to divine Reason with this absolute production of qualities, which, to the extent that they emanate from our subjectivity, congeal before our eyes into impermeable objectivities.

Since the creation can find its fulfillment only in reading, since the artist must entrust to another the job of carrying out what he has begun, since it is only through the consciousness of the reader that he can regard himself as essential to his work, all literary work is an appeal. To write is to make an appeal to the reader that he lead into objective existence the revelation which I have undertaken by means of language. And if it should be asked *to what* the writer is appealing, the answer is simple. As the sufficient reason for the appearance of the aesthetic object is never found either in the book (where we find merely solicitations to produce the object) or in the author's mind, and as his subjectivity, which he cannot get away from, cannot give a reason for the act of leading into objectivity, the appearance of the work of art is a new event which cannot *be explained* by anterior data. And since this directed creation is an absolute beginning, it is therefore brought about by the freedom of the reader, and by what is purest in that freedom. Thus, the writer appeals to the reader's freedom to collaborate in the production of his work.

It will doubtless be said that all tools address themselves to our freedom since they are the instruments of a possible action, and that the work of art is not unique in that. And it is true that the tool is the congealed outline of an operation. But it remains on the level of the hypothetical imperative. I may use a hammer to nail up a case or to hit my neighbor over the head. Insofar as I consider it in itself, it is not an appeal to my freedom; it does not put me face to face with it; rather, it aims at using it by substituting a set succession of traditional procedures for the free invention of means. The book does not serve my freedom; it requires it. Indeed, one cannot address himself to freedom as such by means of constraint, fascination, or entreaties. There is only one way of attaining it; first, by recognizing it, then, having confidence in it, and finally, requiring of it an act, an act in its own name, that is, in the name of the confidence that one brings to it.

Thus, the book is not, like the tool, a means for any end whatever; the end to which it offers itself is the reader's freedom. And the Kantian expression "finality without end" seems to me quite inappropriate for designating the work of art. In fact, it implies that the aesthetic object presents only the appearance of a finality and is limited to soliciting the free and ordered play of the imagination. It forgets that the imagination of the spectator has not only a regulating function, but a constitutive one. It does not play; it is called upon to recompose the beautiful object beyond the traces left by the artist. The imagination can not revel in itself any more than can the other functions of the mind; it is always on the outside, always engaged in an enterprise. There would be finality without end if some object offered such a set ordering that it would lead us to suppose that it has one even though we can not ascribe one to it. By defining the beautiful in this way one can — and this is Kant's aim — liken the beauty of art to natural beauty, since a flower, for example, presents so much symmetry, such harmonious colors, and such regular curves, that one is immediately tempted to seek a finalist explanation for all these properties and to see them as just so many means at the disposal of an unknown end. But that is exactly the error. The beauty of nature is in no way comparable to that of art. The work of art *does not have* an end; there we agree with Kant. But the reason is that it is an end. The Kantian formula does not account for the appeal which resounds at the basis of each painting, each statue, each book. Kant believes that the work of art first exists as fact and that it is then seen. Whereas, it exists only if one *looks* at it and if it is first pure appeal, pure exigence to exist. It is not an instrument whose existence is manifest and whose end is undetermined. It presents itself as a task to be discharged; from the very beginning it places itself on the level of the categorical imperative. You are perfectly free to leave that book on the table. But if you open it, you assume responsibility for it. For freedom is not experienced by its enjoying its free subjective functioning, but in a creative act required by an imperative. This absolute end, this imperative which is transcendent yet acquiesced in, which freedom itself adopts as its own, is what we call a value. The work of art is a value because it is an appeal.

If I appeal to my readers so that we may carry the enterprise which I have begun to a successful conclusion, it is self-evident that I consider him as a pure freedom, as an unconditioned activity; thus, in no case can I address myself to his passivity, that is, try to *affect* him, to communicate to him, from the very first, emotions of fear, desire, or anger. There are, doubtless, authors who concern themselves solely with arousing these emotions because they are foreseeable, manageable, and because they have at their disposal sure-fire means for provoking them. But it is also true that they are reproached for this kind of thing, as Euripides has been since antiquity because he had children appear on the stage. Freedom is alienated in the state of passion; it is abruptly engaged in partial enterprises; it loses sight of its task which is to produce an absolute end. And the book is no longer anything but a means for feeding hate or desire. The writer should not seek to *overwhelm;* otherwise he is in contradiction with himself; if he wishes to *make demands* he must propose only the task to be fulfilled. Hence, the character of pure presentation which appears essential to the work of art. The reader must be able to make a certain aesthetic withdrawal. This is what Gautier foolishly confused with "art for art's sake" and the Parnassians with the imperturbability of the artist. It is simply a matter of precaution, and Genet more justly calls it the author's politeness toward the reader. But that does not mean that the writer makes an appeal to some sort of abstract and conceptual freedom. One certainly creates the aesthetic object with feelings; if it is touching, it appears through our tears; if it is comic, it will be recognized by laughter. However, these feelings are of a particular kind. They have their origin in freedom; they are loaned. The belief which I accord the tale is freely assented to. It is a Passion, in the Christian sense of the word, that is, a freedom which resolutely puts itself into a state of passivity to obtain a certain transcendent effect by this sacrifice. The reader renders himself credulous; he descends into credulity which, though it ends by enclosing him like a dream, is at every moment conscious of being free. An effort is sometimes made to force the writer into this dilemma: "Either one believes in your story, and it is intolerable, or one does not believe in it, and it is ridiculous." But the argument is absurd because the characteristic of aesthetic consciousness is to be a belief by means of engagement, by oath, a belief sustained by fidelity to one's self and to the author, a perpetually renewed choice to believe. I can awaken at every moment, and I know it; but I do not want to; reading is a free dream. So that all feelings which are exacted on the basis of this imaginary belief are like particular modulations of my freedom. Far from absorbing or masking it, they are so many different ways it has chosen to reveal itself to itself. Raskolnikov, as I have said, would only be a shadow, without the mixture of repulsion and friendship which I feel for him and which makes him live. But, by a reversal which is the characteristic of the imaginary object, it is not his behavior which excites my indignation or esteem, but my indignation and esteem which give consistency and objectivity to his behavior.

Thus, the reader's feelings are never dominated by the object, and as no external reality can condition them, they have their permanent source in freedom; that is, they are all generous — for I call a feeling generous which has its origin and its end in freedom. Thus, reading is an exercise in generosity, and what the writer requires of the reader is not the application of an abstract freedom but the gift of his whole person, with his passions, his prepossessions, his sympathies, his sexual temperament, and his scale of values. Only this person will give himself generously; freedom goes through and through him and comes to transform the darkest masses of his sensibility. And as activity has rendered itself passive in order for it better to create the object, vice-versa, passivity becomes an act; the man who is reading has raised himself to the highest degree. That is why we see people who are known for their toughness shed tears at the recital of imaginary misfortunes; for the moment they have become what they would have been if they had not spent their lives hiding their freedom from themselves.

Thus, the author writes in order to address himself to the freedom of readers, and he requires it in order to make his work exist. But he does not stop there; he also requires that they return this confidence which he has given them, that they recognize his creative freedom, and that they in turn solicit it by a symmetrical and inverse appeal. Here there appears the other dialectical paradox of reading; the more we experience our freedom, the more we recognize that of the other; the more he demands of us, the more we demand of him.

When I am enchanted with a landscape, I know very

well that it is not I who create it, but I also know that without me the relations which are established before my eyes among the trees, the foliage, the earth, and the grass would not exist at all. I know that I can give no reason for the appearance of finality which I discover in the assortment of hues and in the harmony of the forms and movements created by the wind. Yet, it exists; there it is before my eyes, and I can make *there be* being only if being already *is*. But even if I believe in God, I can not establish any passage, unless it be purely verbal, between the divine, universal solicitude and the particular spectacle which I am considering. To say that He made the landscape in order to charm me or that He made me the kind of person who is pleased by it is to take a question for an answer. Is the marriage of this blue and that green deliberate? How can I know? The idea of a universal providence is no guarantee of any particular intention, especially in the case under consideration, since the green of the grass is explained by biological laws, specific constants, and geographical determinism, while the reason for the blue of the water is accounted for by the depth of the river, the nature of the soil and the swiftness of the current. The assorting of the shades, if it is willed, can only be something *thrown into the bargain;* it is the meeting of two causal series, that is to say, at first sight, a fact of chance. At best, the finality remains problematic. All the relations we establish remain hypotheses; no end is proposed to us in the manner of an imperative, since none is expressly revealed as having been willed by a creator. Thus, our freedom is never *called forth* by natural beauty. Or rather, there is an appearance of order in the ensemble of the foliage, the forms, and the movements, hence, the illusion of a calling forth which seems to solicit this freedom and which disappears immediately when one regards it. Hardly have we begun to run our eyes over this arrangement, than the call disappears; we remain alone, free to tie up one color with another or with a third, to set up a relationship between the tree and the water or the tree and the sky, or the tree, the water and the sky. My freedom becomes caprice. To the extent that I establish new relationships, I remove myself further from the illusory objectivity which solicits me. I *muse* about certain motifs which are vaguely outlined by the things; the natural reality is no longer anything but a pretext for musing. Or, in that case, because I have deeply regretted that this arrangement which was momentarily perceived was not offered to me by somebody and consequently is not *real,* the result is that I fix my dream, that I transpose it to canvas or in writing. Thus, I interpose myself between the finality without end which appears in the natural spectacles and the gaze of other men. I transmit it to them. It becomes human by this transmission. Art here is a ceremony of the *gift* and the gift alone brings about the metamorphosis. It is something like the transmission of titles and powers in the matriarchate where the mother does not possess the names, but is the indispensable intermediary between uncle and nephew. Since I have captured this illusion in flight, since I lay it out for other men and have disengaged it and rethought it for them, they can consider it with confidence. It has become intentional. As for me, I remain, to be sure, at the border

53

of the subjective and the objective without ever being able to contemplate the objective ordonnance which I transmit.

The reader, on the contrary, progresses in security. However far he may go, the author has gone farther. Whatever connections he may establish among the different parts of the book — among the chapters or the words — he has a guarantee, namely, that they have been expressly willed. As Descartes says, he can even pretend that there is a secret order among parts which seem to have no connection. The creator has preceded him along the way, and the most beautiful disorders are effects of art, that is, again order. Reading is induction, interpolation, extrapolation, and the basis of these activities rests on the reader's will, as for a long time it was believed that that of scientific induction rested on the divine will. A gentle force accompanies us and supports us from the first page to the last. That does not mean that we fathom the artist's intentions easily. They constitute, as we have said, the object of conjectures, and there is an *experience* of the reader; but these conjectures are supported by the great certainty we have that the beauties which appear in the book are never accidental. In nature, the tree and the sky harmonize only by chance; if, on the contrary, in the novel, the protagonists find themselves in a *certain* tower, in a *certain* prison, if they stroll in a *certain* garden, it is a matter both of the restitution of independent causal series (the character had a certain state of mind which was due to a succession of psychological and social events; on the other hand, he betook himself to a determined place and the layout of the city required him to cross a certain park) and of the expression of a deeper finality, for the park came into existence only *in order to* harmonize with a certain state of mind, to express it by means of things or to put it into relief by a vivid contrast, and the state of mind itself was conceived in connection with the landscape. Here it is causality which is appearance and which might be called "causality without cause," and it is the finality which is the profound reality. But if I can thus in all confidence put the order of ends under the order of causes, it is because by opening the book I am asserting that the object has its source in human freedom.

If I were to suspect the artist of having written out of passion and in passion, my confidence would immediately vanish, for it would serve no purpose to have supported the order of causes by the order of ends. The latter would be supported in its turn by a psychic causality and the work of art would end by re-entering the chain of determinism. Certainly I do not deny when I am reading that the author may be impassioned, nor even that he might have conceived the first plan of his work under the sway of passion. But his decision to write supposes that he withdraws somewhat from his feelings, in short, that he has transformed his emotions into free emotions as I do mine while reading him; that is, that he is in an attitude of generosity.

Thus, reading is a pact of generosity between author and reader. Each one trusts the other; each one counts on the other, demands of the other as much as he demands of himself. For this confidence is itself generosity. Nothing can force the author to believe that his reader will use his freedom; nothing can force the reader to believe that the author has used his. Both of them make a free decision. There is then established a dialectical going-and-coming; when I read, I make demands; if my demands are met, what I am then reading provokes me to demand more of the author, which means to demand of the author that he demand more of me. And, vice-versa, the author's demand is that I carry my demands to the highest pitch. Thus, my freedom, by revealing itself, reveals the freedom of the other.

It matters little whether the aesthetic object is the product of "realistic" art (or supposedly such) or "formal" art. At any rate, the natural relations are inverted; that tree on the first plane of the Cézanne painting first appears as the product of a causal chain. But the causality is an illusion; it will doubtless remain as a proposition as long as we look at the painting, but it will be supported by a deep finality; if the tree is placed in such a way, it is because the rest of the painting *requires* that this form and those colors be placed on the first plane. Thus, through the phenomenal causality, our gaze attains finality as the deep structure of the object, and, beyond finality, it attains human freedom as its source and original basis. Vermeer's realism is carried so far that at first it might be thought to be photographic. But if one considers the splendor of his texture, the pink and velvety glory of his little brick walls, the blue thickness of a branch of woodbine, the glazed darkness of his vestibules, the orange-colored flesh of his faces which are as polished as the stone of holy-water basins, one suddenly feels, in the pleasure that he experiences, that the finality is not so much in the forms or colors as in his material imagination. It is the very substance and temper of the things which here give the forms their reason for being. With this realist we are perhaps closest to absolute creation, since it is in the very passivity of the matter that we meet the unfathomable freedom of man.

The work is never limited to the painted, sculpted, or narrated object. Just as one perceives things only against the background of the world, so the objects represented by art appear against the background of the universe. On the background of the adventures of Fabrice are the Italy of 1820, Austria, France, the sky and stars which the Abbé Blanis consults, and finally the whole earth. If the painter presents us with a field or a vase of flowers, his paintings are windows which are open on the whole world. We follow the red path which is buried among the wheat much farther than Van Gogh has painted it, among other wheat fields, under other clouds, to the river which empties into the sea, and we extend to infinity, to the other end of the world, the deep finality which supports the existence of the field and the earth. So that, through the various objects which it produces or reproduces, the creative act aims at a total renewal of the world. Each painting, each book, is a recovery of the totality of being. Each of them presents this totality to the freedom of the spectator. For this is quite the final goal of art: to recover this world by giving it to be seen as it is, but as if it had its source in human freedom. But, since what the author creates takes on objective reality only in the eyes of the spectator, this recovery is consecrated by the ceremony of the spectacle

— and particularly of reading. We are already in a better position to answer the question we raised a while ago: the writer chooses to appeal to the freedom of other men so that, by the reciprocal implications of their demands, they may re-adapt the totality of being to man and may again enclose the universe within man.

If we wish to go still further, we must bear in mind that the writer, like all other artists, aims at giving his reader a certain feeling that is customarily called aesthetic pleasure, and which I would very much rather call aesthetic joy, and that this feeling, when it appears, is a sign that the work is achieved. It is therefore fitting to examine it in the light of the preceding considerations. In effect, this joy, which is denied to the creator, insofar as he creates, becomes one with the aesthetic consciousness of the spectator, that is, in the case under consideration, of the reader. It is a complex feeling but one whose structures and condition are inseparable from one another. It is identical, at first, with the recognition of a transcendent and absolute end which, for a moment, suspends the utilitarian round of ends-means and means-ends[1], that is, of an appeal or, what amounts to the same thing, of a value. And the positional consciousness which I take of this value is necessarily accompanied by the non-positional consciousness of my freedom, since my freedom is manifested to itself by a transcendent exigency. The recognition of freedom by itself is joy, but this structure of non-thetical consciousness implies another: since, in effect, reading is creation, my freedom

---

1. In *practical life* a means may be taken for an end as soon as one searches for it, and each end is revealed as a means of attaining another end.

does not only appear to itself as pure autonomy but as creative activity, that is, it is not limited to giving itself its own law but perceives itself as being constitutive of the object. It is on this level that the phenomenon specifically is manifested, that is, a creation wherein the created object is given *as object* to its creator. It is the sole case in which the creator gets any enjoyment out of the object he creates. And the word enjoyment which is applied to the positional consciousness of the work read indicates sufficiently that we are in the presence of an essential structure of aesthetic joy. This positional enjoyment is accompanied by the non-positional consciousness of being essential in relation to an object perceived as essential. I shall call this aspect of aesthetic consciousness the feeling of security; it is this which stamps the strongest aesthetic emotions with a sovereign calm. It has its origin in the authentication of a strict harmony between subjectivity and objectivity. As, on the other hand, the aesthetic object is properly the world insofar as it is aimed at through the imaginary, aesthetic joy accompanies the positional consciousness that the world is a value, that is, a task proposed to human freedom. I shall call this the aesthetic modification of the human project, for, as usual, the world appears as the horizon of our situation, as the infinite distance which separates us from ourselves, as the synthetic totality of the given, as the undifferentiated ensemble of obstacles and implements — but never as a demand addressed to our freedom. Thus, aesthetic joy proceeds to this level of the consciousness which I take of recovering and internalizing that which is non-ego par excellence, since I transform the given into an imperative ai.. the fact into a value. The world is *my task*, that is, the essential and freely accepted function of my freedom is to make that unique and absolute object which is the universe come into being in an unconditioned movement. And, thirdly, the preceding structures imply a pact between human freedoms, for, on the one hand, reading is a confident and exacting recognition of the freedom of the writer, and, on the other hand, aesthetic pleasure, as it is itself experienced in the form of a value, involves an absolute exigence in regard to others; every man, insofar as he is a freedom, feels the same pleasure in reading the same work. Thus, all mankind is present in its highest freedom; it sustains the being of a world which is both *its* world and the "external" world. In aesthetic joy the positional consciousness is an *image-making* consciousness of the world in its totality both as being and having to be, both as totally ours and totally foreign, and the more ours as it is the more foreign. The non-positional consciousness *really* envelops the harmonious totality of human freedoms insofar as it makes the object of a universal confidence and exigency.

To write is thus both to disclose the world and to offer it as a task to the generosity of the reader. It is to have recourse to the consciousness of others in order to make one's self be recognized as *essential* to the totality of being; it is to wish to live this essentiality by means of interposed persons; but, on the other hand, as the real world is revealed only by action, as one can feel himself in it only by exceeding it in order to change it, the novelist's universe would lack thickness if it were not dis-

60

covered in a movement to transcend it. It has often been observed that an object in a story does not derive its density of existence from the number and length of the descriptions devoted to it, but from the complexity of its connections with the different characters. The more often the characters handle it, take it up, and put it down, in short, go beyond it toward their own ends, the more real will it appear. Thus, of the world of the novel, that is, the totality of men and things, we may say that in order for it to offer its maximum density the disclosure-creation by which the reader discovers it must also be an imaginary engagement in the action; in other words, the more disposed one is to change it, the more alive it will be. The error of realism has been to believe that the real reveals itself to contemplation, and that consequently one could draw an impartial picture of it. How could that be possible, since the very perception is partial, since by itself the naming is already a modification of the object? And how could the writer, who wants himself to be essential to this universe, want to be essential to the injustice which this universe comprehends? Yet, he must be; but if he accepts being the creator of injustices, it is in a movement which goes beyond them toward their abolition. As for me who read, if I create and keep alive an unjust world, I can not help making myself responsible for it. And the author's whole art is bent on obliging me to *create* what he *discloses,* therefore to compromise myself. So both of us bear the responsibility for the universe. And precisely because this universe is supported by the joint effort of our two freedoms, and because the author, with me as medium, has attempted to integrate it into the human, it must appear truly *in itself,* in its very marrow, as being shot through and through with a freedom which has taken human freedom as its end, and if it is not really the city of ends that it ought to be, it must at least be a stage along the way; in a word, it must be a becoming and it must always be considered and presented not as a crushing mass which weighs us down, but from the point of view of its going beyond toward that city of ends. However bad and hopeless the humanity which it paints may be, the work must have an air of generosity. Not, of course, that this generosity is to be expressed by means of edifying discourses and virtuous characters; it must not even be premeditated, and it is quite true that fine sentiments do not make fine books. But it must be the very warp and woof of the book, the stuff out of which the people and things are cut; whatever the subject, a sort of essential lightness must appear everywhere and remind us that the work is never a natural datum, but an *exigence* and a *gift.* And if I am given this world with its injustices, it is not so that I might contemplate them coldly, but that I might animate them with my indignation, that I might disclose them and create them with their nature as injustices, that is, as abuses to be suppressed. Thus, the writer's universe will only reveal itself in all its depth to the examination, the admiration, and the indignation of the reader; and the generous love is a promise to maintain, and the generous indignation is a promise to change, and the admiration a promise to imitate; although literature is one thing and morality a quite different one, at the heart of the aesthetic imperative we discern the moral imperative. For, since the one who writes recognizes, by the very fact that he takes the trouble to write, the freedom of his readers, and since the one who reads, by the mere fact of his opening the book, recognizes the freedom of the writer, the work of art, from whichever side you approach it, is an act of confidence in the freedom of men. And since readers, like the author, recognize this freedom only to demand that it manifest itself, the work can be defined as an imaginary presentation of the world insofar as it demands human freedom. The result of which is that there is no "gloomy literature", since, however dark may be the colors in which one paints the world, he paints it only so that free men may feel their freedom as they face it. Thus, there are only good and bad novels. The bad novel aims to please by flattering, whereas the good one is an exigence and an act of faith. But above all, the unique point of view from which the author can present the world to those freedoms whose concurrence he wishes to bring about is that of a world to be impregnated always with more freedom. It would be inconceivable that this unleashing of generosity provoked by the writer could be used to authorize an injustice, and that the reader could enjoy his freedom while reading a work which approves or accepts or simply abstains from condemning the subjection of man by man. One can imagine a good novel being written by an American Negro even if hatred of the whites were spread all over it, because it is the freedom of his race that he demands through this hatred. And, as he invites me to assume the attitude of generosity, the moment I feel myself a pure freedom I can not bear to identify myself with a race of oppressors. Thus, I require of all freedoms that they demand the liberation of colored people against the white race and against myself insofar as I am a part of it, but nobody can suppose for a moment that it is possible to write a good novel in praise of anti-Semitism.[1] For, the moment I feel that my freedom is indissolubly linked with that of all other men, it can not be demanded of me that I use it to approve the enslavement of a part of these men. Thus, whether he is an essayist, a pamphleteer, a satirist, or a novelist, whether he speaks only of individual passions or whether he attacks the social order, the writer, a free man addressing free men, has only one subject — freedom.

Hence, any attempt to enslave his readers threatens him in his very art. A blacksmith can be affected by fascism in his life as a man, but not necessarily in his craft; a writer will be affected in both, and even more in his craft than in his life. I have seen writers, who before the war, called for fascism with all their hearts, smitten with sterility at the very moment when the Nazis were loading them with honors. I am thinking of Drieu la Rochelle in particular; he was mistaken, but he was sincere. He proved it. He had agreed to direct a Nazi-inspired review. The first few months he reprimanded, rebuked, and lectured his countrymen. No one answered

1. This last remark may arouse some readers. If so, I'd like to know a single good novel whose express purpose was to serve oppression, a single good novel which has been written against Jews, negroes, workers, or colonial people. "But if there isn't any, that's no reason why someone may not write one some day." But you then admit that you are an abstract theoretician. You, not I. For it is in the name of your abstract conception of art that you assert the possibility of a fact which has never come into being, whereas I limit myself to proposing an explanation for a recognized fact.

him because no one was free to do so. He became irritated; he no longer *felt* his readers. He became more insistent, but no sign appeared to prove that he had been understood. No sign of hatred, nor of anger either; nothing. He seemed disoriented, the victim of a growing distress. He complained bitterly to the Germans. His articles had been superb; they became shrill. The moment arrived when he struck his breast; no echo, except among the bought journalists whom he despised. He handed in his resignation, withdrew it, again spoke, still in the desert. Finally, he kept still, gagged by the silence of others. He had demanded the enslavement of others, but in his crazy mind he must have imagined that it was voluntary, that it was still free. It came; the man in him congratulated himself mightily, but the writer could not bear it. While this was going on, others, who, happily, were in the majority, understood that the freedom of writing implies the freedom of the citizen. One does not write for slaves. The art of prose is bound up with the only regime in which prose has meaning, democracy. When one is threatened, the other is too. And it is not enough to defend them with the pen. A day comes when the pen is forced to stop, and the writer must then take up arms. Thus, however you might have come to it, whatever the opinions you might have professed, literature throws you into battle. Writing is a certain way of wanting freedom; once you have begun, you are engaged, willy-nilly.

Engaged in what? Defending freedom? That's easy to say. Is it a matter of acting as guardian of ideal values like Benda's clerk before the betrayal,[1] or is it concrete,

---

1. The reference here is to Benda's *La Trahison dés clercs*, translated into English as *The Treason of the Intellectuals.*—Translator's note.

everyday freedom which must be protected by our taking sides in political and social struggles? The question is tied up with another one, one very simple in appearance but which nobody ever asks himself: "For whom does one write?"

# III

## FOR WHOM DOES ONE WRITE?

At first sight, there doesn't seem to be any doubt: one writes for the universal reader, and we have seen, in effect, that the exigency of the writer is, as a rule, addressed to *all* men. But the preceding descriptions are ideal. As a matter of fact the writer knows that he speaks for freedoms which are swallowed up, masked, and unavailable; and his own freedom is not so pure; he has to clean it. It is dangerously easy to speak too readily about eternal values; eternal values are very, very fleshless. Even freedom, if one considers it *sub specie aeternitatis*, seems to be a withered branch; for, like the sea, there is no end to it. It is nothing else but the movement by which one perpetually uproots and liberates himself. There is no given freedom. One must win an inner victory over his passions, his race, his class, and his nation and must conquer other men along with himself. But what counts in this case is the particular form of the obstacle to surmount, of the resistance to overcome. That is what gives form to freedom in each circumstance. If the writer has chosen, as Benda has it, to talk drivel, he can speak in fine, rolling periods of that eternal freedom which National Socialism, Stalinist communism, and the capitalist democracies all lay claim to. He won't disturb anybody; he won't address anybody. Everything he asks for is granted him in advance. But it is an abstract dream. Whether he wants to or not, and even if he has his eyes on eternal laurels, the writer is speaking to his contemporaries and brothers of his class and race.

As a matter of fact, it has not been sufficiently observed that a work of the mind is by nature *allusive*. Even if the author's aim is to give the fullest possible representation of his object, there is never any question as to whether he is telling *everything*. He knows far more than he tells. This is so because language is elliptical. If I want to let my neighbor know that a wasp has gotten in by the window, there is no need for a long speech. "Watch out!" or "Hey!" — a word is enough, a gesture — as soon as he sees it, everything is clear. Imagine a phonograph record reproducing for us, without comment, the everyday conversations of a household in Provins or Angoulême — we wouldn't understand a thing; the *context* would be lacking, that is, memories and perceptions in common, the situation and the enterprises of the couple; in short, the world such as each of the speakers knows it to appear to the other.

The same with reading: people of a same period and collectivity, who have lived through the same events, who have raised or avoided the same questions, have the same taste in their mouth; they have the same complicity, and there are the same corpses among them. That is why it is not necessary to write so much; there are key-words. If I were to tell an audience of Americans about the German occupation, there would have to be a great deal of analysis and precaution. I would waste twenty pages in dispelling preconceptions, prejudices, and legends. Afterward, I would have to be sure of my position at every step; I would have to look for images and symbols in American history which would enable them to understand ours; I would always have to keep in mind the difference between our old man's pessimism and their childlike optimism. If I were to write about the same subject for Frenchmen, we are "entre nous." For example, it would be enough to say: "A concert of German military music in the band-stand of a public garden;" everything is there; a raw spring day, a park in the provinces, men with shaven skulls blowing away at their brasses, blind and deaf passers-by who quicken their steps, two or three sullen-looking listeners under the trees, this useless serenade to France which drifts off into the sky, our shame and our anguish, our anger, and our pride too. Thus, the reader I am addressing is neither Micromégas nor L'Ingénu; nor is he God the Father either. He has not the ignorance of the noble savage to whom everything has to be explained on the basis of principles; he is not a spirit or a *tabula rasa*. Neither has he the omniscience of an angel or of the Eternal Father. I reveal certain aspects of the universe to him; I take advantage of what he knows to attempt to teach him what he does not know. Suspended between total ignorance and all-knowingness, he has a definite stock of knowledge which varies from moment to moment and which is enough to reveal his *historicity*. In actual fact, he is not an instantaneous consciousness, a pure timeless affirmation of freedom, nor does he soar above history; he is involved in it.

Authors too are historical. And that is precisely the reason why some of them want to escape from history by a leap into eternity. The book, serving as a go-between, establishes a historical contact among the men who are steeped in the same history and who likewise contribute to its making. Writing and reading are two facets of the same historical fact, and the freedom to which the writer invites us is not a pure abstract consciousness of being free. Strictly speaking, it *is not*; it wins itself in a historical situation; each book proposes a concrete liberation on the basis of a particular alienation. Hence, in each one there is an implicit recourse to institutions, customs, certain forms of oppression and conflict, to the wisdom and the folly of the day, to lasting passions and passing stubbornness, to superstitions and recent victories of common sense, to evidence and ignorance, to particular modes of reasoning which the sciences have made fashionable and which are applied in all domains, to hopes, to fears, to habits of sensibility, imagination, and even perception, and finally, to customs and values which have been handed down, to a whole world which the author and the reader have in common. It is this familiar world which the writer animates and penetrates with his freedom. It is on the basis of this world that the reader must bring about his concrete liberation; it is alienation, situation, and history. It is this world which I must change or preserve for myself and others. For if the immediate aspect of freedom is negativity, we know that it is not a matter of the abstract power of saying no, but of a concrete negativity which retains within itself (and is completely colored by) what it denies. And since the freedoms of the author and reader seek and affect each other through a world, it can just as well be said that the author's choice of a certain aspect of the world determines the reader and, vice-versa, that it is by choosing his reader that the author decides upon his subject.

Thus, all works of the mind contain within themselves the image of the reader for whom they are intended. I could draw the portrait of Nathanaël on the basis of *Les Nourritures terrestres*: I can see that the alienation from which he is urged to free himself is the family, the real-estate he owns or will own by inheritance, the utilitarian project, a conventional moralism, a narrow theism; I also see that he is cultured and has leisure, since it would be absurd to offer Ménalque as an example to an unskilled laborer, a man out of work, or an American negro; I know that he is not threatened by any external danger, neither by hunger, war, nor class or racial oppression; the only danger is that of being the victim of his own milieu. Therefore, he is a white rich Aryan, the heir of a great bourgeois family which lives in a period which is still relatively stable and easy, in which the ideology of the possessing class is barely beginning to decline, exactly the Daniel de Fontanin whom Roger Martin du Gard later presented to us as an enthusiastic admirer of André Gide.

To take a still more recent example, it is striking that *The Silence of the Sea*, a work written by a man who was a member of the resistance from the very beginning and whose aim is perfectly evident, was received with hostility in the émigré circles of New York, London, and sometimes even Algiers, and they even went so far as to tax its author with collaboration. The reason is that Ver-

71

cors did not aim at *that* public. In the occupied zone, on the other hand, nobody doubted the author's intentions or the efficacy of his writing; he was writing for us. As a matter of fact, I do not think that one can defend Vercors by saying that his German is real or that his old Frenchman and French girl are real. Koestler has written some very fine pages about this question; the silence of the two French characters has no psychological verisimilitude; it even has a slight taste of anachronism; it recalls the stubborn muteness of Maupassant's patriotic peasants during another occupation, *another* occupation with other hopes, other anguish, and other customs. As to the German officer, his portrait does not lack life, but, as is self-evident, Vercors, who, at the time, refused to have any contact with the army of occupation, did it "without a model," by combining the probable elements of this character. Thus, it is not in the name of *truth* that these images should be preferred to those which Anglo-Saxon propaganda was shaping each day. But for a Frenchman of continental France Vercors' story, in 1941, was *effective*. When the enemy is separated from you by a barrier of fire, you have to judge him as a whole, as the incarnation of evil; all war is a Manicheism. It is therefore understandable that the English newspapers did not waste their time distinguishing the wheat from the chaff in the German army. But, vice-versa, the conquered and occupied populations, who mingled with their conquerors, relearned by familiarization and the effects of clever propaganda to consider them as men. Good men and bad men; good *and* bad at the same time. A work which in '41 would have presented the German soldiers to them as ogres would have made them laugh and would have failed in its purpose.

As early as the end of '42 *The Silence of the Sea* had lost its effectiveness; the reason is that the war was starting again on our soil. On one side, underground propaganda, sabotage, derailment of trains, and acts of violence; and on the other, curfew, deportations, imprisonment, torture, and execution of hostages. An invisible barrier of fire once again separated Germans and Frenchmen. We no longer wished to know whether the Germans who plucked out the eyes and ripped off the nails of our friends were accomplices or victims of Nazism; it was no longer enough to maintain a lofty silence before them; besides, they would not have tolerated it. At this turn of the war it was necessary to be either for them or against them. In the midst of bombardments and massacres, of burned villages and deportations, Vercors' story seemed like an idyll; it had lost its public. Its public was the man of '41 humiliated by defeat but astonished at the studied courtesy of the occupant, desiring peace, terrified by the spectre of Bolshevism and misled by the speeches of Pétain. It was in vain to present the Germans to this man as bloodthirsty brutes. On the contrary, you had to admit to him that they might be polite and even likable, and since he had discovered with surprise that most of them were "men like us," he had to be re-shown that even if such were the case, fraternizing was impossible, that the more likable they seemed, the more unhappy and impotent they were, and that it was necessary to fight against a régime and an ideology even if the men who brought it to us did not seem bad. And, in short, as one

73

was addressing a passive crowd, as there were still rather few important organizations, and as these showed themselves to be highly precautious in their recruiting, the only form of opposition that could be required of the population was silence, scorn, and an obedience which was forced and which showed it.

Thus, Vercors' story defined its public; by defining it, it defined itself. It wanted to combat within the mind of the French bourgeoisie of 1941 the effects of Pétain's interview with Hitler at Montoire. A year and a half after the defeat it was alive, virulent, and effective. In a half-century it will no longer excite anyone. An ill-informed public will still read it as an agreeable and somewhat languid tale about the war of 1939. It seems that bananas have a better taste when they have just been picked. Works of the mind should likewise be eaten on the spot.

One might be tempted to accuse any attempt to explain a work of the mind by the public to which it is addressed for its vain subtlety and its indirect character. Is it not more simple, direct, and rigorous to take the condition of the author himself as the determining factor? Ought one not be satisfied with Taine's notion of the "milieu"? I answer that the explanation by the milieu is, in effect, *determinative*: the milieu *produces* the writer; that is why I do not believe in it. On the contrary, the public calls to him, that is, it puts questions to his freedom. The milieu is a *vis a tergo*; the public, on the contrary, is a waiting, an emptiness to be filled in, *an aspiration*, figuratively and literally. In a word, it is the *other*. And I am so far from rejecting the explanation of the work by the situation of the man that I have always considered the project of writing as the free exceeding of a certain human and *total* situation. In which, moreover, it is not different from other undertakings. Étiemble in a witty but superficial article writes,[1] "I was going to revise my little dictionary when chance put three lines of Jean-Paul Sartre right under my nose: 'In effect, for us the writer is neither a Vestal nor an Ariel. Do what he may, he's in the thick of it, marked and compromised down to his deepest refuge.' To be in the thick of it, up to the ears. I recognized, in a way, the words of Blaise Pascal: 'We are embarked.' But at once I saw engagement lose all its value, reduced suddenly to the most ordinary of facts, the fact of the prince and the slave, to the human condition."

That's what I said all right. But Étiemble is being silly. If every man is embarked, that does not at all mean that he is fully conscious of it. Most men pass their time in hiding their engagement from themselves. That does not necessarily mean that they attempt evasions by lying, by artificial paradises, or by a life of make-believe. It is enough for them to dim their lanterns, to see the foreground without the background and, vice-versa, to see the ends while passing over the means in silence, to refuse solidarity with their kind, to take refuge in the spirit of pompousness, to remove all value from life by considering it from the point of view of someone who is dead, and at the same time, all horror from death by fleeing it in the banality of everyday existence, to per-

1. Etiemble: "Happy the writers who die for something." *Combat*, January 24, 1947.

suade themselves, if they belong to an oppressing class, that they are escaping their class by the loftiness of their feelings, and, if they belong to the oppressed, to conceal from themselves their complicity with oppression by asserting that one can remain free while in chains if one has a taste for the inner life. Writers can have recourse to all this just like anyone else. There are some, and they are the majority, who furnish a whole arsenal of ruses to the reader who wants to go on sleeping quietly.

I shall say that a writer is engaged when he tries to achieve the most lucid and the most complete consciousness of being embarked, that is, when he causes the engagement of immediate spontaneity to advance, for himself and others, to the reflective. The writer is, par excellence, a mediator and his engagement is mediation. But, if it is true that we must account for his work on the basis of his condition, it must also be borne in mind that his condition is not only that of a man in general but precisely that of a writer as well. Perhaps he is a Jew, and a Czech, and of peasant family, but he is a Jewish *writer*, a Czech *writer* and of rural stock. When, in another article, I tried to define the situation of the Jew, the best I could do was this: "The Jew is a man whom other men consider as a Jew and who is obliged to choose himself on the basis of the situation which is made for him." For there are qualities which come to us solely by means of the judgment of others. In the case of the writer, the case is more complex, for no one is obliged to choose himself as a writer. Hence, freedom is at the origin. I am an author, first of all, by my free project of writing. But at once it follows that I become a man whom other men consider as a writer, that is, who has to respond to a certain demand and who has been invested whether he likes it or not, with a certain social function. Whatever game he may want to play, he must play it on the basis of the representation which others have of him. He may want to modify the character that one attributes to the man of letters in a given society; but in order to change it, he must first slip into it. Hence, the public intervenes, with its customs, its vision of the world, and its conception of society and of literature within that society. It surrounds the writer, it hems him in, and its imperious or sly demands, its refusals and its flights, are the given facts on whose basis a work can be constructed.

Let us take the case of the great negro writer, Richard Wright. If we consider only his condition as a *man*, that is, as a Southern "nigger" transported to the North, we shall at once imagine that he can only write about Negroes or Whites *seen through the eyes of Negroes*. Can one imagine for a moment that he would agree to pass his life in the contemplation of the eternal True, Good, and Beautiful when ninety percent of the negroes in the South are practically deprived of the right to vote? And if anyone speaks here about the treason of the clerks, I answer that there are no clerks among the oppressed. Clerks are necessarily the parasites of oppressing classes or races. Thus, if an American negro finds that he has a vocation as a writer, he discovers his subject at the same time. He is the man who sees the whites from the outside, who assimilates the white culture from the outside, and each of whose books will show the alienation of the black race within American society. Not objectively, like the realists, but passionately, and in a way that will compromise his reader. But this examination leaves the nature of his work undetermined; he might be a pamphleteer, a blues-writer, or the Jeremiah of the Southern negroes.

If we want to go further, we must consider his public. To whom does Richard Wright address himself? Certainly not to the universal man. The essential characteristic of the notion of the universal man is that he is not involved in any particular age, and that he is no more and no less moved by the lot of the negroes of Louisiana than by that of the Roman slaves in the time of Spartacus. The universal man can think of nothing but universal values. He is a pure and abstract affirmation of the inalienable right of man. But neither can Wright think of intending his books for the white racists of Virginia or South Carolina whose minds are made up in advance and who will not open them. Nor to the black peasants of the bayous who can not read. And if he seems to be happy about the reception his books have had in Europe, still it is obvious that at the beginning he had not the slightest idea of writing for the European public. Europe is far away. Its indignation is ineffectual and hypocritical. Not much is to be expected from the nations which have enslaved the Indies, Indo-China, and negro Africa. These considerations are enough to define his readers. He is addressing himself to the cultivated negroes of the North and the white Americans of good-will (intellectuals, democrats of the left, radicals, C.I.O. workers).

It is not that he is not aiming through them at all men but it is *through them* that he is thus aiming. Just as one can catch a glimpse of eternal freedom at the horizon of the historical and concrete freedom which it pursues, so the human race is at the horizon of the concrete and historical group of its readers. The illiterate negro peasants and the Southern planters represent a margin of abstract possibilities around its real public. After all, an illiterate may learn to read. *Black Boy* may fall into the hands of the most stubborn of negrophobes and may open his eyes. This merely means that every human project exceeds its actual limits and extends itself step by step to the infinite.

Now, it is to be noted that there is a fracture at the very heart of this *actual public*. For Wright, the negro readers represent subjectivity. The same childhood, the same difficulties, the same complexes: a mere hint is enough for them; they understand with their hearts. In trying to become clear about his own personal situation, he clarifies theirs for them. He mediates, names, and shows them the life they lead from day to day in its immediacy, the life they suffer without finding words to formulate their sufferings. He is their conscience, and the movement by which he raises himself from the immediate to the reflective recapturing of his condition is that of his whole race. But whatever the good-will of the white readers may be, for a negro author they represent the *Other*. They have not lived through what he has lived through. They can understand the negro's condition only by an extreme stretch of the imagination and by relying upon analogies which at any moment may deceive them. On the other hand, Wright does not completely know them. It is only from without that he conceives their proud security and that tranquil certainty, common to all white Aryans, that the world is white and that they own it. The words he puts down on paper have not the same context for whites as for negroes. They must be chosen by guesswork, since he does not know what resonances they will set up in those strange minds. And when he speaks to them, their very aim is changed. It is a matter of implicating them and making them take stock of their responsibilities. He must make them indignant and ashamed.

Thus, each work of Wright contains what Baudelaire would have called "a double simultaneous postulation;" each word refers to two contexts; two forces are applied simultaneously to each phrase and determine the incomparable tension of his tale. Had he spoken to the whites alone, he might have turned out to be more prolix, more didactic, and more abusive; to the negroes alone, still more elliptical, more of a confederate, and more elegiac. In the first case, his work might have come close to satire; in the second, to prophetic lamentations. Jeremiah spoke only to the Jews. But Wright, a writer for a split public, has been able both to maintain and go beyond this split. He has made it the pretext for a work of art.

The writer consumes and does not produce, even if he has decided to serve the community's interests with his pen. His works remain gratuitous; thus no price can be set on their value. Their market value is fixed arbitrarily. In some periods he is pensioned and in others he gets a percentage of the sales of the book. But there is no more common measure between the work of the mind

80

and percentage remuneration in modern society than there was between the poem and the royal pension under the old régime. Actually, the writer is not paid; he is fed, well or badly, according to the period. The system cannot work any differently, for his activity is *useless*. It is not at all *useful*; it is sometimes *harmful* for society to become self-conscious. For the fact is that the useful is defined within the framework of an established society and in relationship to institutions, values, and ends which are already fixed. If society sees itself and, in particular, sees itself as *seen*, there is, by virtue of this very fact, a contesting of the established values of the regime. The writer presents it with its image; he calls upon it to assume it or to change itself. At any rate, it changes; it loses the equilibrium which its ignorance had given it; it wavers between shame and cynicism; it practises dishonesty; thus, the writer gives society *a guilty conscience*; he is thereby in a state of perpetual antagonism toward the conservative forces which are maintaining the balance he tends to upset. For the transition to the mediate which can be brought about only by a negation of the immediate is a perpetual revolution.

Only the governing classes can allow themselves the luxury of remunerating so unproductive and dangerous an activity, and if they do so, it is a matter both of tactics and of misapprehension. Misapprehension for the most part: free from material cares, the members of the governing élite are sufficiently detached to want to have a reflective knowledge of themselves. They want to retrieve themselves, and they charge the artist with presenting them with their image without realizing that he will then make them assume it. A tactic on the part of some who, having recognized the danger, pension the artist in order to control his destructive power. Thus, the writer is a parasite of the governing "élite." But, functionally, he moves in opposition to the interests of those who keep him alive.[1] Such is the original conflict which defines his condition.

Sometimes the conflict is obvious. We still talk about the courtiers who made the success of the *Marriage of Figaro* though it sounded the death-knell of the régime. Other times, it is masked, because to name is to show, and to show is to change. And as this activity of contestation, which is harmful to the established interests, ventures, in its very modest way, to concur in a change of régime, as, on the other hand, the oppressed classes have neither the leisure nor the taste for reading, the objective aspect of the conflict may express itself as an antagonism between the conservative forces, or the real public of the writer, and the progressive forces, or the virtual public.

In a classless society, one whose internal structure would be permanent revolution, the writer might be a mediator *for all*, and his contestation on principle might precede or accompany the changes in fact. In my opinion this is the deeper meaning we should give to the notion of *self-criticism*. The expanding of the real public up to the limits of his virtual public would bring about within his mind a reconciliation of hostile tendencies. Literature, entirely liberated, would represent *negativity* insofar as it is a necessary moment in reconstruction. But

---

1. To-day his public is spread out. He sometimes runs into a hundred thousand copies. A hundred thousand copies sold, that makes four hundred thousand readers. Thus, for France, one out of a hundred in the population.

to my knowledge this type of society does not for the moment exist, and it may be doubted whether it is possible. Thus, the conflict remains. It is at the origin of what I would call the writer's ups and downs and his bad conscience.

It is reduced to its simplest expression when the virtual public is practically nil and when the writer, instead of remaining on the margin of the privileged class, is absorbed by it. In that case literature identifies itself with the ideology of the directing class; reflection takes place within the class; contestation deals with details and is carried on in the name of uncontested principles. For example, that is what happened in Europe about the twelfth century; the clerk wrote exclusively for clerks. But he could keep a good conscience because there was a divorce between the spiritual and the temporal. The Christian Revolution brought in the spiritual, that is, the spirit itself, as a negativity, a contestation, and a transcendence, a perpetual construction, beyond the realm of Nature, of the *anti-natural* city of freedoms. But it was necessary that this universal power of surpassing the object be first encountered as an object, that this perpetual negation of Nature appear, in the first place, as nature, that this faculty of perpetually creating ideologies and of leaving them behind along the way be embodied, to begin with, in a particular ideology. In the first centuries of our era the spiritual was a captive of Christianity, or, if you prefer, Christianity was the spiritual itself but *alienated*. It was the spirit made object. Hence, it is evident that instead of appearing as the common and forever renewed experience of all men, it manifested itself at first as the specialty of a few. Medieval society had spiritual needs, and, to serve them, it set up a body of specialists who were recruited by co-optation. To-day we consider reading and writing as human rights and, at the same time, as means for communicating with others which are almost as natural and spontaneous as oral language. That is why the most uncultured peasant is a potential reader. In the time of the clerks, they were techniques which were reserved strictly for professionals. They were not practised for their own sake, like spiritual exercises. Their aim was not to obtain access to that large and vague humanism which was later to be called "the humanities." They were means solely of preserving and transmitting Christian ideology. To be able to read was to have the necessary tool for acquiring knowledge of the sacred texts and their innumerable commentaries; to be able to write was to be able to comment. Other men no more aspired to possess these professional techniques than we aspire to-day to acquire that of the cabinet-maker or the palaeographer if we practice other professions. The barons counted on the clerks to produce and watch over spirituality. By themselves they were incapable of exercising control over writers as the public does to-day, and they were unable to distinguish heresy from orthodox beliefs if they were left without help. They got excited only when the pope had recourse to the secular arm. Then they pillaged and burned everything, but only because they had confidence in the pope, and they never turned up their noses at a chance to pillage. It is true that the ideology was ultimately intended for them, for them and the people, but it was communicated to them orally by preachings, and the church very early made use of a simpler language than writing: the image. The sculpture of the cloisters and the cathedrals, the stained-glass windows, the paintings, and the mosaics speak of God and the Holy Story. The clerk wrote his chronicles, his philosophical works, his commentaries, and his poems on the margin of this vast illustrating enterprise of faith. He intended them for his peers; they were controlled by his superiors. He did not have to be concerned with the effects which his works would produce upon the masses, since he was assured in advance that they would have no knowledge of them. Nor did he want to introduce remorse into the conscience of a feudal plunderer or caitiff; violence was unlettered. Thus, for him it was neither a question of reflecting its own image back to the temporal, nor of taking sides, nor of disengaging the spiritual from historical experience by a continuous effort. Quite the contrary, as the writer was of the Church, as the Church was an immense spiritual college which proved its dignity by its resistance to change, as history and the temporal were one and spirituality was radically distinct from the temporal, as the aim of his clerkship was to maintain this distinction, that is, to maintain itself as a specialized body in the face of the century, as, in addition, the economy was so divided up and as means of communication were so few and slow that events which occurred in one province had no effect upon the neighboring province and as a monastery could enjoy its individual peace, like the hero of the *Acharnians,* while its country was at war, the writer's mission was to prove his autonomy by delivering himself to the exclusive contemplation of the Eternal. He incessantly affirmed the

85

Eternal's existence and demonstrated it precisely by the fact that his only concern was to regard it. In this sense, he realized, in effect, the ideal of Benda, but one can see under what conditions: spirituality and literature had to be alienated, a particular ideology had to triumph, a feudal pluralism had to make the isolation of the clerks possible, virtually the whole population had to be illiterate, and the only public of the writer could be the college of other writers. It is inconceivable that one can practise freedom of thought, write for a public which coincides with the restricted collectivity of specialists, and restrict oneself to describing the content of eternal values and *a priori* ideas. The good conscience of the medieval clerk flowered on the death of literature.

However, in order for writers to preserve this happy conscience it is not quite necessary that their public be reduced to an established body of professionals. It is enough for them to be steeped in the ideology of the privileged classes, to be completely permeated with it, and to be unable even to conceive any others. But in this case their function is modified; they are no longer asked to be the *guardians* of dogma but merely not to make themselves its detractors. As a second example of the adherence of writers to established ideology, one might, I believe, choose the French seventeenth century.

The secularization of the writer and his public was in process of being completed in that age. It certainly had its origin in the expansive force of the written thing, its monumental character, and the appeal to freedom which is hidden away in any work of the mind. But external circumstances contributed, such as the development of education, the weakening of the spiritual power, and the appearance of new ideologies which were expressly intended for the temporal. However, secularization does not mean universalization. The writer's public still remained strictly limited. Taken as a whole, it was called *society*, and this name designated a fraction of the court, the clergy, the magistracy, and the rich bourgeoisie. Considered individually, the reader was called a "gentleman" (*honnête homme*) and he exercised a certain function of censorship which was called *taste*. In short, he was both a member of the upper classes and a specialist. If he criticized the writer, it was because he himself could write. The public of Corneille, Pascal, and Descartes was Mme. de Sévigné, the Chevalier de Méré, Madame de Grignan, Madame de Rambouillet, and Saint-Évremonde. To-day the public, in relation to the writer, is in a state of passivity: it waits for ideas or a new art form to be imposed upon it. It is the inert mass wherein the idea will assume flesh. Its means of control is indirect and negative; one can not say that it gives its opinion; it simply buys or does not buy the book; the relationship between author and reader is analogous to that of male and female: reading has become a simple means of information and writing a very general means of communication. In the seventeenth century being able to write already meant really being able to write well. Not that Providence divided the gift of style equally among all men, but because the reader, if not strictly identical with the writer, was a potential writer. He belonged to a parasitical élite for whom the art of writing was, if not a profession, at least the mark of its superiority. One read because he could write; with a little luck he might have been able to write what he read. The public was active; productions of the mind were really *submitted* to it. It judged them by a scale of values which it helped maintain. A revolution analogous to romanticism is not conceivable in this period because there would have to have been the concurrence of an indecisive mass, which one surprises, overwhelms, and suddenly animates by revealing to it ideas or feelings of which it was ignorant, and which, lacking firm convictions, constantly requires being ravished and fecundated. In the seventeenth century convictions were unshakeable; the religious ideology went hand in hand with a political ideology which the temporal itself secreted; no one publicly questioned the existence of God or the divine right of kings. "Society" had its language, its graces, and its ceremonies which it expected to find in the books it read. Its conception of time, too. As the two historical facts which it constantly pondered — original sin and redemption — belonged to a remote past, as it was also from this past that the great governing families drew their pride and the justification of their privileges, as the future could bring nothing new, since God was too perfect to change, and since the two great earthly powers, the Church and the Monarchy, aspired only to immutability, the active element of temporality was the past, which is itself a phenomenal degradation of the Eternal; the present is a perpetual sin which can find an excuse for itself only if it reflects, with the least possible unfaithfulness, the image of a completed era. For an idea to be received, it must prove its antiquity; for a work of art to please, it must have been inspired by an ancient model. Again we find writers expressly making themselves the guardians of this ideology. There were still great clerks who belonged to the Church and who had no other concern than to defend dogma. To them were added the "watchdogs" of the temporal, historians, court poets, jurists, and philosophers who were concerned with establishing and maintaining the ideology of the absolute monarchy. But we see appearing at their side a third category of writers, strictly secular, who, for the most part, *accepted* the religious and political ideology of the age without thinking that they were bound to prove it or preserve it. They did not write about it, they accepted it implicitly. For them, it was what we called a short time ago the context or the ensemble of the presuppositions common to readers and author which are necessary to make the writings of the latter intelligible to the former. In general, they belonged to the bourgeoisie; they were pensioned by the nobility. As they consumed without producing, and as the nobility did not produce either but lived off the work of others, they were the parasites of a parisitic class. They no longer lived in a college but formed an implicit corporation in that highly integrated society, and to remind them constantly of their collegiate origin and their former clerkship the royal power chose some of them and grouped them in a sort of symbolic college, the French Academy. Fed by the king and read by an élite, they were concerned solely with responding to the demands of this limited public. They had as good or almost as good a conscience as the twelfth-century clerks. It is impossible to speak of a virtual public as distinguished from a real public in this age. La Bruyère happened to speak *about* peasants, but he did not speak *to* them, and if he took note of their misery, it was not for the sake of drawing an argument against the ideology he accepted, but in the name of that ideology: it was a disgrace for enlightened monarchs and good Christians. Thus, one spoke about the masses above their heads and without even conceiving the notion that one might help them become self-conscious. And the homogeneity of the public banished all contradiction from the authors' souls. They were not pulled between real but detestable readers and readers who were virtual and desirable but out of reach; they did not ask themselves questions about their role in the world, for the writer questions himself about his mission only in ages when it is not clearly defined and when he must invent or re-invent it, that is, when he notices, beyond the élite who read him, an amorphous mass of possible readers whom he may or may not choose to win, and when he must himself decide, in the event that he has the opportunity to reach them, what his relations with them are to be. The authors of the seventeenth century had a definite function because they addressed an enlightened, strictly limited, and active public which exercised permanent control over them. Unknown by the people, their job was to reflect back its own image to the élite which supported them. But there are many ways of reflecting an image: certain portraits are by themselves contestations because they have been made from without and without passion by a painter who refuses any complicity with his model. However, in order for a writer merely to conceive the idea of drawing a portrait-contestation of his real reader, he must have become conscious of a contradiction between

90

himself and his public, that is, he must come to his readers *from without* and must consider them with astonishment, or he must feel the astonished regard of unfamiliar minds (ethnic minorities, oppressed classes, etc.) weighing upon the little society which he forms with them. But in the seventeenth century, since the virtual public did not exist, since the artist accepted without criticism the ideology of the élite, he made himself an accomplice of his public. No unfamiliar stare came to trouble him in his games. Neither the prose-writer nor even the poet was accursed. They did not have to decide with each work what the meaning and value of literature were, since its meaning and value were fixed by tradition. Well integrated in a hierarchical society, they knew neither the pride nor the anguish of being "different"; in short, they were *classical*. There is classicism when a society has taken on a relatively stable form and when it has been permeated with the myth of its perenniality, that is, when it confounds the present with the eternal and historicity with traditionalism, when the hierarchy of classes is such that the virtual public never exceeds the real public and when each reader is for the writer a qualified critic and a censor, when the power of the religious and political ideology is so strong and the interdictions so rigorous that in no case is there any question of discovering new countries of the mind, but only of putting into shape the *commonplaces* adopted by the élite. in such a way that reading — which, as we have seen, is the concrete relation between the writer and his public — is a ceremony of *recognition* analogous to the bow of salutation, that is, the ceremonious affirmation that author and reader are of

91

the same world and have the same opinions about everything. Thus, each production of the mind is at the same time an act of courtesy, and style is the supreme courtesy of the author toward his reader, and the reader, for his part, never tires of finding the same thoughts in the most diverse of books because these thoughts are his own and he does not ask to acquire others but only to be offered with magnificence those which he already has. Hence, it is in a spirit of complicity that the author presents and the reader accepts a portrait which is necessarily abstract; addressing a parasitical class, he can not show man at work or, in general, the relations between man and external nature. As, on the other hand, there are bodies of specialists who, under the control of the Church and the Monarchy, are concerned with maintaining the spiritual and secular ideology, the writer does not even suspect the importance of economic, religious, metaphysical, and political factors in the constitution of the person; and as the society in which he lives confounds the present with the eternal he can not even imagine the slightest change in what he calls human nature. He conceives history as a series of accidents which affect the eternal man on the surface without deeply modifying him, and if he had to assign a meaning to historical duration he would see in it both an eternal repetition, so that previous events can and ought to provide lessons for his contemporaries, and a process of slight degeneration, since the fundamental events of history are long since *passed* and since, perfection in letters having been attained in Antiquity, his ancient models seem beyond rivalry. And in all this he is once again fully in harmony with his public which considers work as a curse, which does not *feel* its situation in history and in the world for the simple reason that it is privileged and because its only concern is faith, respect for the Monarch, passion, war, death, and courtesy. In short, the image of classical man is purely psychological because the classical public is conscious only of his psychology. Furthermore, it must be understood that this psychology is itself traditionalist, it is not concerned with discovering new and profound truths about the human heart or with setting up hypotheses. It is in unstable societies, when the public exists on several social levels, that the writer, torn and dissatisfied, invents explanations for his anguish. The psychology of the seventeenth century is purely descriptive. It is not based so much upon the author's personal experience as it is the aesthetic expression of what the élite thinks about itself. La Rochefoucauld borrows the form and the content of his maxims from the divertissements of the salons. The casuistry of the Jesuits, the etiquette of the Précieuses, the portrait game, the ethics of Nicole, and the religious conception of the passions are at the origin of a hundred other works. The comedies draw their inspiration from ancient psychology and the plain common sense of the upper bourgeoisie. Society is thoroughly delighted at seeing itself mirrored in them because it recognizes the notions it has about itself; it does not ask to be shown what it is, but it asks rather for a reflection of what it thinks it is. To be sure, some satires are permitted, but it is the élite which, through pamphlets and comedies, carries on, in the name of its morality, the cleansings and the purges necessary for its health. The ridiculous marquis, the litigants, or the Précieuses are never made fun of from a point of view *external* to the governing class; it is always a matter of eccentrics who are inassimilable in a civilized society and who live on the margin of the collective life. The Misanthrope is twitted because he lacks courtesy, Cathos and Madelon, because they have too much. Philaminte goes counter to the accepted ideas about women; the bourgeois gentleman is odious to the rich bourgeois who have a lofty modesty and who know the greatness and the humbleness of their condition, and, at the same time, to the gentlemen because he wants to push his way into the nobility. This internal and, so to speak, physiological satire has no connection with the great satire of Beaumarchais, P.L. Courier, J. Vallès, and Céline; it is less courageous and much more severe because it exhibits the repressive action which the collectivity practices upon the weak, the sick, and the maladjusted. It is the pitiless laughter of a gang of street-urchins at the awkwardness of their butt.

Bourgeois in origin and mores, more like Oronte and Chrysale in his home life than like his brilliant and restless confrères of 1780 or 1830, yet accepted in the Society of the Great and pensioned by them, slightly unclassed from above, yet convinced that talent is no substitute for birth, docile to the reprimands of the clergy, respectful of the royal power, happy to occupy a modest place in the immense structure of which the Church and the Monarchy are the pillars, somewhat above the merchants and the scholars, below the nobles and the clergy, the writer practises his profession with a good conscience, convinced that he has come too late, that everything has been said, and that the only proper thing to do is to re-say it agreeably. He conceives the glory which awaits him as a feeble reflection of hereditary titles and if he expects it to be eternal it is because he does not even suspect that the society of his readers may be overthrown by social changes. Thus, the permanence of the royal family seems to him a guarantee of that of his renown.

Yet, almost in spite of himself, the mirror which he modestly offers to his readers is magical: it enthralls and compromises. Even though everything has been done to offer them only a flattering and complying image, more subjective than objective and more internal than external, this image remains none the less a work of art, that is, it has its basis in the freedom of the author and is an appeal to the freedom of the reader. Since it is beautiful, it is made of glass; aesthetic distance puts it out of reach. Impossible to be delighted with it, to find any comfortable warmth in it, any discrete indulgence. Even though it is made up of the commonplaces of the age and that smug complacency which unite contemporaries like an umbilical cord, it is supported by a freedom and thereby another kind of objectivity. It is *itself*, to be sure, that the élite finds in the mirror, but itself as it would see itself if it went to the very extremes of severity. It is not congealed into an object by the gaze of the Other, for neither the peasant nor the working-man has yet become the *Other* for it, and the art of reflective presentation which characterizes the art of the seventeenth century is a strictly internal process; however, it pushes to the limits each one's

95

efforts to see into himself clearly; it is a perpetual *cogito*. To be sure, it does not call idleness, oppression, or parasitism into question, because these aspects of the governing class are revealed only to observers who place themselves outside of it; hence, the image which is reflected back to it is strictly psychological. But spontaneous behavior, by passing to the reflective state, loses its innocence and the excuse of immediacy: it must be assumed or changed. It is, to be sure, a world of courtesy and ceremony which is offered to the reader, but he is is already emerging from this world since he is invited to know it and to recognize himself in it. In this sense, Racine was not wrong when he said in regard to *Phèdre* that "the passions are presented before your eyes only to show all the disorder of which they are the cause". On condition that one does not take that to mean that his express purpose was to inspire a horror of love. But to paint passion is already to go beyond it, already to shed it. It is not a matter of chance that, about the same time, philosophers were suggesting the idea of curing one's self of it by knowledge. And as the reflective practice of freedom when confronted by the passions is usually adorned with the name of *morals,* it must be recognized that the art of the seventeenth century is eminently a moralizing art. Not that its avowed aim is to teach virtue, nor that it is poisoned by the good intentions which produce bad literature, but by the mere fact that it quietly offers the reader his own image, it makes it unbearable for him. Moralizing: this is both a definition and a limit. It is not moralizing *only;* if it proposes to man that he transcend the psychological toward the moral, it is because it regards religious, metaphysical, political, and social problems as solved; but its action is none the less "orthodox." As it confounds universal man with the particular men who are in power, it does not dedicate itself to the liberation of any concrete category of the oppressed; however, the writer, though completely assimilated by the oppressing class, is by no means its accomplice; his work is unquestionably a liberator since its effect, within this class, is to free man from himself.

Up to this point we have been considering the case in which the writer's potential public was nil, or just about, and in which his real public was not torn by any conflict. We have seen that he could then accept the current ideology with a good conscience and that he launched his appeals to freedom within the ideology itself. If the potential public suddenly appears, or if the real public is broken up into hostile factions everything changes. We must now consider what happens to literature when the writer is led to reject the ideology of the ruling classes.

The eighteenth century was the palmy time, unique in history, and the soon-to-be-lost paradise, of French writers. Their social condition had not changed. Bourgeois in origin, with very few exceptions, they were unclassed by the favors of the great. The circle of their real readers had grown perceptibly larger because the bourgeoisie had begun to read, but they were still unknown to the "lower" classes, and if the writers spoke of them more often than did La Bruyère and Fénelon, they never addressed them, even in spirit. However, a profound upheaval had broken their public in two; they had to satisfy contradictory demands. Their situation was characterized from the beginning by *tension*. This tension was manifested in a very particular way. The governing class had in fact lost confidence in its ideology. It had put itself into a position of defense; it tried, to a certain extent, to retard the diffusion of new ideas, but it could not keep from being penetrated by these ideas. It understood that its religious and political principles were the best instruments for establishing its power, but the fact is that as it saw them only as instruments, it ceased to believe in them completely. *Pragmatic* truth had replaced revealed truth. If censorship and prohibitions were more visible, they covered up a secret weakness and a cynicism of despair. There were no more *clerks;* church literature was empty apologetics, a fist holding on to dogmas which were breaking loose; it was turning against freedom; it addressed itself to respect, fear, and self-interest, and by ceasing to be a free appeal to free men, it was ceasing to be literature. This distraught élite turned to the genuine writer and asked him to do the impossible, not to spare his severity, if he was bent on it, but to breathe at least a bit of freedom into a wilting ideology, to address himself to his readers' reason and to persuade them to adopt dogmas which, with time, had become irrational. In short, to turn propagandist without ceasing to be a writer. But it was playing a losing game. Since its principles were no longer a matter of immediate and unformulated evidence and since it had to *present* them to the writer so that he might come to their defense, since there was no longer any question of saving them for their own sake but rather of maintaining order, it contested their validity by its very effort to re-establish them. The writer who consented to buttress this shaky ideology at least *consented* to do so, and this voluntary adherence to principles which, in the past, had governed minds without being noticed now freed him from them. He was already going beyond them. In spite of himself he was emerging into solitude and freedom. The bourgeoisie, on the other hand, which constituted what in Marxist terms is called the rising class, was trying at this same time to disengage itself from the ideology that was being imposed upon it and to construct one better suited to its own purpose.

Now, this "rising class," which was soon to claim the right to participate in affairs of State, was subject only to *political* oppression. Confronted with a ruined nobility, it was in process of very calmly attaining economic preeminence. It already had money, culture, and leisure. Thus, for the first time an oppressed class was presenting itself to the writer as a real public. But the conjunction was still more favorable; for this awakening class, which was reading and trying to think, had not yet produced an organized revolutionary party which would secrete its own ideology as did the Church in the Middle Ages. The writer was not yet wedged, as we shall see that he was later to be, between the dying ideology of a declining class and the rigorous ideology of the rising class. The bourgeoisie wanted light; it felt vaguely that its thought was alienated, and it wanted to become conscious of itself. One could probably find some traces of organization: materialist societies, groups of intellectuals, free masonry. But they were chiefly associations for inquiry which were waiting for ideas rather than producing them. To be sure, a form of popular and spontaneous writing was spreading, the secret and anonymous tract. But this literature of amateurs did not compete with the professional writer but rather goaded and solicited him by informing him about the confused aspirations of the collectivity. Thus, the bourgeoisie—as opposed to a public of half-specialists, which with difficulty held on to its position and which was always recruited at the Court and from the upper circles of society—offered the rough draft of a mass public. In regard to literature, it was in a state of relative *passivity* since it had no experience in the art of writing, no preconceived opinion about style and literary genres, and was awaiting everything, form and content, from the genius of the writer.

Solicited by both sides, the writer found himself between the two hostile factions of his public as the arbiter of their conflict. He was no longer a clerk; the ruling class was not the only one supporting him. It is true that it was still pensioning him, but it was the bourgeoisie which was buying his books. He was collecting at both ends. His father had been a bourgeois and his son would be one; one might thus be tempted to see in him a bourgeois more gifted than others but similarly oppressed, a man who had attained knowledge of his state under the pressure of historical circumstances, in short, an inner mirror by means of which the whole bourgeoisie became conscious of itself and its demands. But this would be a superficial view. It has not been sufficiently pointed out that a class can acquire class consciousness only if it sees itself from within and without at the same time; in other words, if it profits by external competition; that is where the intellectuals, the perpetually unclassed, come into the picture.

The essential characteristic of the eighteenth-century writer was precisely an objective and subjective unclassing. Though he still remembered his bourgeois attachments, yet the favor of the great drew him away from his milieu; he no longer felt any concrete solidarity with his cousin the lawyer or his brother the village curé because he had privileges which they had not. It was from the court and nobility that he borrowed his manners and the very graces of his style. Glory, his dearest hope and his consecration, had become for him a slippery and ambiguous notion; a fresh idea of glory was rising up in which a writer was truly rewarded if an obscure doctor in Bruges or a brief-less lawyer in Rheims devoured his books almost in secret.

But the diffuse recognition of this public which he hardly knew only half touched him. He had received from his elders a traditional conception of fame. According to this conception, it was the monarch who consecrated his genius. The visible sign of his success was for Catherine or Frederick to invite him to their table. The recompense given to him and the dignities conferred from above did not yet have the official impersonality of the prizes and decorations awarded by our republics. They retained the quasi-feudal character of man to man relations. And since he was, above all, an eternal consumer in a society of producers, a parasite of a parasitic class, he treated money like a parasite. He did not *earn* it since there was no common measure between his work and his remuneration; he only *spent* it. Therefore, even if he was poor, he lived in luxury. Everything was a luxury to him, including, and in fact particularly so, his writing. Yet, even in the king's chamber he retained a rough force, a potent vulgarity; Diderot, in the heat of a philosophical conversation, pinched the thigh of the Empress of Russia until the blood flowed. And then, if he went too far, he could always be made to feel that he was only a scribbler. The life of Voltaire, from his beating, his imprisonment, and his flight to London, to the insolence of the King of Prussia was a succession of triumphs and humiliations. At times the writer enjoyed the passing favors of a marquise, but he married his maid or a bricklayer's daughter. Hence, his mind, as well as his public, was torn apart. But this did not cause him to suffer; on the contrary, this original contradiction was the source of his pride. He thought that he had no obligations to anyone, that he could choose his friends and opponents, and that it was enough for him to take his pen in hand to free himself from the conditioning of milieu, nation, or class. He flew, he soared, he was pure thought, pure observation. He chose to write to vindicate his unclassing which he assumed and transformed into solitude. From the outside, he contemplated the great with the eyes of the bourgeois and the bourgeois with the eyes of the nobility, and he retained enough complicity with both to understand them equally from within. Hence, literature, which up to then had been only a conservative and purifying function of an integrated society, became conscious in him and by him of its autonomy. Placed by an extreme chance between confused aspirations and an ideology in ruins—like the writer between the bourgeoisie, the Court, and the Church—literature suddenly asserted its independence. It was no longer to reflect the common-places of the collectivity; it identified itself with Mind, that is, with the permanent power of forming and criticizing ideas.

Of course, this taking over of literature by itself was abstract and almost purely formal, since the literary works were not the concrete expression of any class; and as the writers began by rejecting any deep solidarity with the milieu from which they came as well as the one which adopted them, literature became confused with Negativity, that is, with doubt, refusal, criticism, and contestation. But as a result of this very fact, it led to the setting up, against the ossified spirituality of the Church, the rights of a new spirituality, one in movement, which was no longer identified with any ideology and which manifested itself as the power of continually surpassing the given, whatever it might be. When, in the shelter of the structure of the very Christian monarchy, it was imitating wonderful models, it hardly fussed about truth because truth was only a very crude and very concrete quality of the ideology which had been nourishing it; for the dogmas of the Church, to be true or, quite simply, to be, was all one, and truth could not be conceived apart from the system. But now that spirituality had become this abstract movement which cut through all ideologies and then left them along the wayside like empty shells, truth, in its turn, was disengaged from all concrete and particular philosophy; it was revealed in its abstract independence; it became the regulating idea of literature and the distant limit of the critical movement.

Spirituality, literature, and truth: these notions were

103

bound up in that abstract and negative moment of becoming self-conscious. Their instrument was analysis, a negative and critical method which perpetually dissolves concrete data into abstract elements and the products of history into combinations of universal concepts. An adolescent chooses to write in order to escape an oppression from which he suffers and a solidarity he is ashamed of; as soon as he has written a few words, he thinks he has escaped from his milieu and class and from all milieus and all classes and that he has broken through his historical situation by the mere fact that he has attained reflective and critical knowledge. Above the confusion of those bourgeois and nobles, locked up in their particular age by their prejudices, he has, on taking up his pen, discovered himself as a timeless and unlocalized mind, in short, as *universal man*. And literature, which has delivered him, is an abstract function and an a priori power of human nature; it is the movement whereby at every moment man frees himself from history; in short, it is the exercise of freedom.

In the seventeenth century, by choosing to write a man embraced a definite profession, with the tricks of the trade, its rules and customs, its rank in the hierarchy of the professions. In the eighteenth century, the molds were broken; everything remained to be done; works of the mind, instead of being put together according to established norms and more or less by luck, were each a particular invention and were a kind of decision of the author regarding the nature, value, and scope of Belles Lettres; each one brought its own rules and the principles by which it was to be judged; each one aspired to engage the whole of literature and to cut out new paths. It is not by chance that the worst works of the period are also those which claimed to be the most traditional; tragedy and epic were the exquisite fruits of an integrated society; in a collectivity which was torn apart, they could subsist only in the form of survivals and pastiches.

What the eighteenth-century writer tirelessly demanded in all his works was the right to practise an anti-historical reason against history, and in this sense all he did was to reveal the essential requirements of abstract literature. He was not concerned with giving his readers a clearer class consciousness. Quite the contrary, the urgent appeal which he addressed to his bourgeois public was an invitation to forget humiliations, prejudices, and fears; the one he directed to his noble public was a solicitation to strip itself of its pride of caste and its privileges. As he had made himself universal, he could have only universal readers, and what he required of the freedom of his contemporaries was that they cut their historical ties in order to join him in universality.

What is the origin of this miracle by which, at the very moment he was setting up abstract freedom against concrete oppression and Reason against History, he was going along in the very direction of historical development? First, the bourgeoisie, by a tactic which was characteristic of it and which it was to repeat in 1830 and 1848, joined forces, on the eve of taking power, with those oppressed classes which were not in a condition to push their demands. And since the bonds which united social groups so different from one another could only be very general and very abstract, it aimed not so much at acquiring a clear consciousness of itself, which would have opposed it to the workmen and peasants, as to have its right to lead the opposition recognized on the grounds that it was in a better position to let the established powers know the demands of universal human nature. On the other hand, the revolution being prepared was a *political* one; there was no revolutionary ideology and no organized party. The bourgeoisie wanted to be enlightened; it wanted the ideology which for centuries had mystified and alienated man to be liquidated. There would be time later on to replace it. For the time being, it aimed at freedom of opinion as a step toward political power. Hence, by demanding *for himself* and *as a writer* freedom of thinking and of expressing his thought, the author necessarily served the interests of the bourgeois class. No more was asked of him and there was nothing more he could do. In later periods, as we shall see, the writer could demand his freedom to write with a bad conscience; he might be aware that the oppressed classes wanted something other than that freedom. Freedom of thinking could then appear as a privilege; in the eyes of some it could pass for a means of oppression, and the position of the writer risked becoming untenable. But on the eve of the Revolution he enjoyed an extraordinary opportunity, that is, it was enough for him to defend his profession in order to serve as a guide to the aspirations of the rising class.

He knew it. He considered himself a guide and a spiritual chief. He took chances. As the ruling élite, which grew increasingly nervous, lavished its graces upon him one day only to have him locked up the next, he had none of that tranquillity, that proud mediocrity, which his predecessors had enjoyed. His glorious and eventful life, with its sunlit crests and its dizzying steeps, was that of an adventurer. The other evening I was reading the dedication of Blaise Cendrars' *Rum*: "To the young people of today who are tired of literature, to prove to them that a novel can also be an act," and I thought that we are quite unfortunate and quite guilty, since we have to prove what in the eighteenth century was self-evident. A work of the mind was then doubly an act since it produced ideas which were to lead to social upheavals and since it exposed its author to danger. And this act, whatever the book we may be considering, was always defined in the same way; it was a *liberator*. And, doubtless, in the seventeenth century too, literature had a liberating function, though one which remained veiled and implicit. In the time of the Encyclopedists, it was no longer a question of freeing the gentleman from his passions by reflecting them back to him without complaisance, but of helping with the pen to bring about the political freedom simply of man. The appeal which the writer addressed to his bourgeois public was, whether he meant it or not, an incitement to revolt; the one which he directed to the ruling class was an invitation to lucidity, to critical self-examination, to the giving up of its privileges. The condition of Rousseau was much like that of Richard Wright's writing for both enlightened negroes and whites. Before the nobility he *bore witness* and at the same time was inviting his fellow commoners to become conscious of themselves. It was not only the taking of the Bastille which his writings and those of Diderot and Condorcet were preparing at long range; it was also the night of August the fourth.

And as the writer thought that he had broken the bonds which united him to his class of origin, as he spoke to his readers from above about universal human nature, it seemed to him that the appeal he made to them and the part he took in their misfortunes were dictated by pure generosity. To write is to give. In this way he accepted and excused what was unacceptable in his situation as a parasite in an industrious society; this was also how he became conscious of that absolute freedom, that gratuity, which characterize literary creation. But though he constantly had in view universal man and the abstract rights of human nature, there is no reason to believe that he was an incarnation of the clerk as Benda has described him. Since his position was, in essence, *critical,* he certainly had to have *something* to criticize; and the objects which first presented themselves to criticism were the institutions, superstitions, traditions, and acts of a traditional government.

In other words, as the walls of Eternity and the Past which had supported the ideological structure of the seventeenth century cracked and gave way, the writer perceived a new dimension of temporality in its purity: the Present. The Present, which preceding centuries had sometimes conceived as a perceptible figuration of Eternity and sometimes as a degraded emanation of Antiquity. He had only a confused notion of the future, but he knew that the fleeting hour which he was living was unique and that it was his, that it was in no way inferior to the most magnificent hours of Antiquity, since they too had begun by being the present. He knew that it was his chance and that he must not waste it. That was why he considered the fight he had to wage not so much as a preparation for the society of the future but rather as a short-term enterprise, one of immediate efficacy. It was *this* institution that had to be denounced and right now, *that* superstition that had to be destroyed immediately, *that* particular injustice that had to be rectified. This impassioned sense of the present saved him from idealism; he did not confine himself to contemplating the eternal ideas of Freedom or Equality. For the first time since the Reformation, writers intervened in public life, protested against an unjust decree, asked for the review of a trial, and, in short, decided that the spiritual was in the street, at the fair, in the market place, at the tribunal, and that it was by no means a matter of turning away from the temporal, but, on the contrary, that one had to come back to it incessantly and go on beyond it in each particular circumstance.

Thus, the overthrow of his public and the crisis of the European consciousness had invested the writer with a new function. He conceived literature to be the permanent practice of magnanimity. He still submitted to the strict and severe control of his peers, but below him he caught a glimpse of an unformed and passionate waiting, a more feminine, more undifferentiated kind of desire which freed him from their censorship. He had disembodied the spiritual and had separated his cause from that of a dying ideology; his books were free appeals to the freedom of his readers.

The political triumph of the bourgeoisie which writers had so eagerly desired convulsed their condition from top to bottom and put the very essence of literature into question. It might be said that the result of all their efforts was merely a preparation for their certain ruin. There is no doubt that by identifying the cause of belles-lettres with that of political democracy they helped the bourgeoisie come to power, but by the same token they ran the risk of seeing the disappearance of the object of their demands, that is, the constant and almost the only subject of their writing. In short, the miraculous harmony which united the essential demands of literature with that of the oppressed bourgeoisie was broken as soon as both were realized. So long as millions of men were burning to be able to express their feelings it was fine to demand the right to write freely and to examine everything, but once freedom of thought and confession and equality of political rights were gained, the defense of literature became a purely formal game which no longer amused anyone; something else had to be found.

Now, at the same time writers had lost their privileged position whose origin had been the split which had torn apart their public and which had allowed them to have a foot in both camps. These two halves had knitted together; the bourgeoisie had absorbed the nobility or very nearly. Authors had to meet the demands of a unified public. There was no hope of getting away from their class of origin. Born of bourgeois parents, read and paid by bourgeois, they had to remain bourgeois; the bourgeoisie had closed around them like a prison. It was to take them a century to get over their keen regret for the flighty and parasitic class which had indulged them out of caprice and whom they had remorselessly undermined in their role of double agent. It seemed to them that they had killed the goose which laid the golden eggs. The bourgeoisie introduced new forms of oppression; however, it was not parasitic. Doubtless, it had taken over the means of work, but it was highly diligent in regulating the production and distribution of its products. It did not conceive literary work as a gratuitous and disinterested creation but as a paid service.

The justifying myth of this industrious and unproductive class was *utilitarianism*; in one way or another the function of the bourgeois was that of intermediary between producer and consumer; it was the *middle term* raised to omnipotence. Thus, in the indissoluble yoke of means and end, he had chosen to give primary importance to the means. The end was implied; one never looked it in the face but passed over it in silence. The goal and dignity of a human life was to spend itself in the ordering of means. It was not *serious* to occupy oneself without intermediary in producing an absolute end. It was as if one aspired to see God face to face without the help of the Church. The only enterprises to be credited were those whose end was the perpetually withdrawing horizon of an infinite series of means. If the work of art entered the utilitarian round, if it hoped to be taken seriously, it had to descend from the heaven of unconditioned ends and resign itself to becoming useful in its turn, that is, to presenting itself as a means of ordering means. In particular, as the bourgeois was not quite sure of himself, because his power was not based on a decree of Providence, literature had to help it feel bourgeois by divine right. Thus, after having been the bad conscience of the privileged in the

111

eighteenth century it ran the risk in the nineteenth century of becoming the good conscience of an oppressing class.

Well and good, if the writer could have kept that spirit of free criticism which in the preceding century had been his fortune and his pride. But his public was opposed to that. So long as the bourgeoisie had been struggling against the privileges of the nobility it had given assent to destructive negativity. But now that it had power, it passed on to construction and asked to be helped in constructing. Contestation had remained possible within the religious ideology because the believer referred his obligations and the articles of faith back to the will of God. He thereby established a concrete and feudal person to person bond with the Almighty. This recourse to the free divine arbiter introduced, although God was perfect and chained to His perfection, an element of gratuity into Christian ethics and consequently a bit of freedom into literature. The Christian hero was always Jacob wrestling with the angel; the saint *contested* the divine will even if he did so in order to submit to it even more narrowly. But bourgeois ethics did not derive from Providence; its universal and abstract procedures were inscribed in things; they were not the effect of a sovereign and quite amiable but personal will, they rather resembled the increate laws of physics. At least, so one supposed, for it was not prudent to look at them too closely. The serious man kept from examining them precisely because their origin was obscure. Bourgeois art would either be a means or would not be; it would forbid itself to lay

112

hands on principles, for fear they might collapse[1], and to probe the human heart too deeply for fear of finding disorder in it. Its public feared nothing so much as talent, that gay and menacing madness which uncovers the disturbing roots of things by unforeseeable words and which, by repeated appeals to freedom, stirs the still more disturbing roots of men. *Facility* sold better; it was talent in leash, turned against itself, the art of reassuring readers by harmonious and expected discourse, in a tone of good fellowship, that man and the world were quite ordinary, transparent, without surprises, without threats, and without interest.

There was more: as the only relationship which the bourgeois had with natural forces was through intermediaries, as material reality appeared to him in the form of manufactured products, as he was surrounded as far as the eye could see by an already humanized world which reflected back to him his own image, as he limited himself to gleaning on the surface of things the meaning that other men had put forward, as his job was essentially that of handling abstract symbols, words, figures, plans, and diagrams for determining methods whereby his employees would share in consumer's goods, as his culture, quite as much as his trade, inclined him to consider ideas, he was convinced that the universe was reducible to a system of ideas; he dissolved effort, difficulty, needs, oppression, and wars into ideas; there was no evil, only pluralism; certain ideas lived in a free state; they had to be

---

1. Dostoievsky's famous "If God does not exist, all is permissible" is the terrible revelation which the bourgeoisie has forced itself to conceal during the one hundred fifty years of its reign.

integrated into the system. Thus, he conceived human progress as a vast movement of assimilation; ideas assimilated each other and so did minds. At the end of this immense digestive process, thought would find its unification and society its total integration.

Such optimism was at the opposite extreme of the writer's conception of his art; the artist needs an unassimilable matter because beauty is not resolved into ideas. Even if he is a prose-writer and assembles signs, his style will have neither grace nor force if it is not sensitive to the materiality of the word and its irrational resistances. And if he wishes to build the universe in his work and to support it by an inexhaustible freedom, the reason is that he radically distinguishes things from thought. His freedom and the thing are homogeneous only in that both are unfathomable, and if he wishes to readapt the desert or the virgin forest to the Mind, he does so not by transforming them into ideas of desert and forest, but by having Being sparkle as Being, with its opacity and its coefficient of adversity, by the indefinite spontaneity of Existence. That is why the work of art is not reducible to an idea; first, because it is a production or a reproduction of a *being*, that is of something which never quite allows itself to be *thought*; then, because this being is totally penetrated by an *existence*, that is, by a freedom which decides on the very fate and value of thought. That is also why the artist has always had a special understanding of Evil, which is not the temporary and remediable isolation of an idea, but the irreducibility of man and the world of Thought.

The bourgeois could be recognized by the fact that he

114

denied the existence of social classes and particularly of the bourgeoisie. The gentleman wished to command because he belonged to a caste. The bourgeois based his power and his right to govern on the exquisite ripening which comes from the secular possession of the goods of this world. Moreover, he admitted only synthetic relationships between the owner and the thing possessed; for the rest, he demonstrated by analysis that all men are alike because they are invariant elements of social combinations and because each one of them, whatever his rank, completely possesses *human nature*. Hence, inequalities appeared as fortuitous and passing accidents which could not alter the permanent characteristics of the social atom. There was no proletariat, that is, no synthetic class of which each worker was a passing mode; there were only proletarians, each isolated in his human nature, who were not united by internal solidarity but only by external bonds of resemblance.

The bourgeois saw only *psychological* relations among the individuals whom his analytical propaganda circumvented and separated. That is understandable: as he had no direct hold on things, as his work was concerned essentially with men, it was purely a matter, for him, of pleasing and intimidating. Ceremony, discipline, and courtesy ruled his behavior; he regarded his fellow-men as marionettes, and if he wished to acquire some knowledge of their emotions and character, it was because it seemed to him that each passion was a wire that could be pulled. The breviary of the ambitious bourgeois was "The Art of Making Good;" the breviary of the rich was "The Art of Commanding." Thus, the bourgeoisie considered the writer as an expert. If he started reflecting on the social order, he annoyed and frightened it. All it asked of him was to share his practical experience of the human heart. So, as in the seventeenth century, literature was reduced to psychology. All the same, the psychology of Corneille, Pascal and Vauvenargues was a cathartic appeal to freedom. But the merchant distrusted the freedom of the people he dealt with and the prefect that of the sub-prefect. All they wanted was to be provided with infallible recipes for winning over and dominating. Man had to be governable as a matter of course and by modest means. In short, the laws of the heart had to be rigorous and without exceptions. The bourgeois bigwig no more believed in human freedom than the scientist believes in a miracle. And as his ethics were utilitarian, the chief motive of his psychology was self-interest. For the writer it was no longer a matter of addressing his work as an appeal to absolute freedoms, but of exhibiting the psychological laws which determined him to readers who were likewise determined.

Idealism, psychologism, determinism, utilitarianism, the spirit of seriousness, that was what the bourgeois writer had to reflect to his public first of all. He was no longer asked to restore the strangeness and opacity of the world, but to dissolve it into elementary subjective impressions which made it easier to digest — nor to discover the most intimate movements of his heart at the very depths of his freedom, but to bring his "experience" face to face with that of his readers. All his works were at once inventories of bourgeois appurtenances, psychological reports of an expert which invariably tended to ground the

116

rights of the élite and to show the wisdom of institutions, and handbooks of civility. The conclusions were decided in advance; the degree of depth permitted to the investigation was also established in advance; the psychological motives were selected; the very style was regulated. The public feared no surprise. It could buy with its eyes closed. But literature had been assassinated. From Émile Augier to Marcel Prévost and Edmond Jaloux, including Dumas *fils*, Pailleron, Ohnet, Bourget, and Bordeaux, authors were found to do the job and, if I may say so, to honor their signature to the very end. It is not by chance that they wrote bad books; if they had talent, they had to hide it.

The best refused. This refusal saved literature but fixed its traits for fifty years. Indeed, from 1848 on, and until the war of 1914, the radical unification of his public led the author to write on principle *against all his readers*. However, he sold his productions, but he despised those who bought them and forced himself to disappoint their wishes. It was taken for granted that it was better to be unknown than famous, that success — if the writer ever got it in his lifetime — was to be explained by a misunderstanding. And if, by chance, the book one published did not offend sufficiently, one added an insulting preface. This fundamental conflict between the writer and his public was an unprecedented phenomenon in literary history. In the seventeenth century the harmony between the man of letters and his readers was perfect; in the eighteenth century the author had two equally real publics at his disposal and could rely upon one or the other as he pleased. In its early stages, romanticism had been

117

a vain attempt to avoid open conflict by restoring this duality and by depending upon the aristocracy against the liberal bourgeoisie. But after 1850 there was no longer any means of covering up the profound contradiction which opposed bourgeois ideology to the requirements of literature. About the same time a virtual public was beginning to take form in the deeper layers of society; it was already waiting to be revealed to itself because the cause of free and compulsory education had made some progress. The Third Republic was soon to sanction the right of all men to read and write. What was the writer going to do? Would he choose the masses over against the élite, and would he attempt to recreate for his own profit the duality of publics?

At first sight, it seemed so. By means of the great movement of ideas which from 1830 to 1848 were brewing in the marginal zones of the bourgeoisie, certain writers had the revelation of their virtual public. They adorned them, under the name of "The People," with mystic graces. It would be the instrument of salvation. But, as much as they loved it, they hardly knew it and above all they did not come from it. Sand was Baronne Dudevant; Hugo, the son of a general of the Empire; even Michelet, the son of a printer, was still far removed from the silk-weavers of Lyons or the textile-weavers of Lille. Their socialism — when they were socialists — was a by-product of bourgeois idealism. And then the people were much rather the subject of certain of their works than their chosen public. Hugo, to be sure, had the rare fortune of penetrating everywhere. He was one of the only, perhaps *the* only one of our writers who was really popular. But the others had incurred the hostility of the bourgeoisie without creating a working-class public in compensation. To convince oneself of this fact all one need do is compare the importance which the bourgeois University accorded to Michelet, an authentic genius and a prose-writer of great class, and to Taine, who was only a cheap pedant, or to Renan, whose "fine style" offers all the examples you want of meanness and ugliness. This purgatory in which the bourgeois class let Michelet vegetate was without compensation; the "people" that he loved read him for a while, and then the success of Marxism pushed him into oblivion. In short, most of these authors were the losers in a revolution that didn't come off. They attached their name and their destiny to it. None of them, except Hugo, really left their mark on literature.

The others, all the others, backed away from the perspective of an unclassing from below which would have made them sink straight down as if a rock had been tied around their necks. They had no lack of excuses: the time wasn't ripe, there was no real bond which attached them to the proletariat, that oppressed class couldn't absorb their work, it didn't know how much it needed them; their decision to defend it had remained abstract; whatever their sincerity might have been, they had "brooded" over miseries which they had understood with their head without feeling them in their heart. Fallen from their class of origin, haunted by the memory of an affluence which they should have refused to accept, they ran the risk of forming "a white-collar proletariat" on the margin of the real proletariat, suspect to the workers and spurned by the bourgeois, whose demands had been dictated by

119

bitterness and resentment rather than large-mindedness and who had ended by turning against both groups.[1] Besides, in the eighteenth century, the necessary liberties required by literature were not distinguished from the political liberties which the citizen wanted to win; all that was necessary for the writer to become a revolutionary was to explore the arbitrary essence of his art and to make himself the interpreter of its formal demands; when the revolution which was in the making was bourgeois, literature was naturally revolutionary because the first discovery which it made of itself revealed to it its connections with political democracy. But the formal liberties which the essayist, the novelist, and the poet were to defend had nothing in common with the deeper needs of the proletariat. The latter was not dreaming of demanding political freedom, which, after all, it did enjoy, and which was only a mystification.[2] As for freedom of thought, for the time being the proletariat was not concerned with it. What it asked for was quite different from these abstract liberties. It wanted the material improvement of its lot, and more deeply, and more obscurely too, the end of man's exploitation by man. We shall see later that these demands were of the same kind made by the art of writing conceived as a concrete and historical phenomenon; that is, as the particular and timely appeal which, by agreeing to historicize himself, a man launches in regard to all mankind to the men of his time.

---

1. This was somewhat the case of Ju'es Valles, though a natural magnanimity constantly struggled within him against bitterness.
2. I am not unaware that workers defended political democracy against Louis Napoleon Bonaparte much more than did the bourgeois, but that was because they thought that by means of it they would be able to bring about structural reforms.

But in the nineteenth century literature had just disengaged itself from religious ideology and refused to serve bourgeois ideology. Thus, it set itself up as being, in principle, independent of any sort of ideology. As a result, it retained its abstract aspect of pure negativity. It had not yet understood that it *was itself* ideology; it wore itself out asserting its autonomy, which no one contested. This amounted to saying that it claimed it had no privileged subject and could treat any matter whatever. There was no doubt about the fact that one might write felicitously about the condition of the working class; but the choice of this subject depended upon circumstances, upon a free decision of the artist. One day one might talk about a provincial bourgeoise, another day, about Carthaginian mercenaries. From time to time, a Flaubert would affirm the identity of form and content, but he drew no practical conclusion from it. Like all his contemporaries, he drew his definition of beauty from what the Winckelmanns and Lessings had said almost a hundred years earlier and which in one way or other boiled down to presenting it as multiplicity in unity. It was a matter of capturing the iridescence of the various and imposing a strict unity upon it by means of style. The "artistic style" of the Goncourts had no other meaning. It was a formal method of unifying and embellishing any materials, even the most beautiful. How could anyone have then conceived that there might be an internal relationship between the demands of the lower classes and the principles of the art of writing? Proudhon seems to have been the only one to have surmised it. And of course Marx. But they were not men of letters. Literature, still com-

121

pletely absorbed by the discovery of its autonomy, was to itself its own subject. It had passed to the reflective period; it tried out its methods, broke its former molds, and tried to determine experimentally its own laws and to forge new techniques. It advanced step by step toward the current forms of the drama and the novel, free verse, and the criticism of language. Had it discovered a specific content, it would have had to tear itself away from its meditation on itself and derive its esthetic norms from the nature of this content.

At the same time, by choosing to write for a virtual public, authors would have had to adapt their art to the capacities of the readers, which would have amounted to determining it according to external demands and not according to its own essence. It would have had to give up some of the exquisite forms of narrative, poetry, and even reasoning, for the sole reason that they would be inaccessible to readers without culture. It seemed, therefore, that literature would be running the risk of relapsing into alienation. Hence, the writer, in all honesty, refused to enslave literature to a public and a determined subject. But he did not perceive the divorce which was taking place between the concrete revolution trying to be born and the abstract games he was indulging in. This time it was the masses who wanted power, and as the masses had no culture or leisure, any would-be literary revolution, by refining its technique, put the works it inspired out of their range and served the interests of social conservatism.

Thus, he had to revert to the bourgeois public. The

writer tried hard to break all relations with it, but by refusing to be unclassed from below, his break was condemned to remain symbolic; he played at it tirelessly; he showed it by his clothes, his food, the way he furnished his home, and the manners he adopted, but he did not do it. It was the bourgeoisie which read him. It was the bourgeoisie alone which maintained him and decided his fame. In vain did he pretend that he was getting perspective in order to consider it as a whole. Had he wanted to judge it, he would first have had to leave it, and there was no other way to leave it than by trying out the interests and way of life of another class. Since he did not bring himself to do this, he lived in a state of contradiction and dishonesty since he both knew and did not want to know *for whom* he was writing. He was fond of speaking of his *solitude*, and rather than assume responsibility for the public which he had slyly chosen, he concocted the notion that one writes for himself alone or for God. He made of writing a metaphysical occupation, a prayer, an examination of conscience, everything but a communication. He frequently likened himself to one possessed, because, if he vomited forth words under the sway of an inner necessity, at least he was not *giving* them. But that did not keep him from carefully polishing his writings. And moreover, he was so far from wishing harm to the bourgeoisie that he did not even dispute its right to govern.

Quite the contrary. Flaubert recognized its right and mentioned it by name, and his correspondence after the Commune, which frightened him so, abounds in disgraceful abuse of the workers.[1] And, as the artist, submerged in his milieu, was unable to judge it from without, as his rejections were ineffectual states of mind, he did not even notice that the bourgeoisie was an oppressing class; in fact, he did not at all consider it as a class, but rather as a natural species, and if he ventured to describe it, he did so in strictly psychological terms.

Thus the bourgeois writer and the damned (*maudit*) writer moved on the same level; their only difference was that the first practised white psychology and the sec-

---

1. I have so often been accused of being unfair to Flaubert that I cannot resist the pleasure of quoting the following texts which anyone can verify in the correspondence:

"Neo-catholicism on one hand and socialism on the other have stultified France. Everything moves between the Immaculate Conception and the workers' lunch-boxes" (1868).

"The first remedy would be to put an end to universal suffrage, the shame of the human mind" (September 1871).

"I'm worth twenty Croisset voters" (1871).

"I have no hatred for the communards for the reason that I don't hate mad dogs" (Croisset, Thursday, 1871).

"I believe that the crowd, the herd, will always be hateful. The only ones important are a small group of spirits, always the same, who pass the torch from hand to hand" (Croisset, September 8, 1871).

"As to the Commune, which is on its last legs, it's the last manifestation of the Middle Ages."

"I hate democracy (at least what it is taken to mean in France), that is, the exaltation of grace to the detriment of justice, the negation of law, in short, anti-sociability."

"The Commune re-instates murderers."

"The people is an eternal minor, and it will always be at the bottom of the scale since it is number, mass, the unbounded."

"It's not important for a lot of peasants to know how to read and no longer listen to their priest, but it's infinitely important that a lot of men like Renan or Littré live and be listened to. Our salvation is now in a *legitimate aristocracy*. I mean by that a majority which will be composed of something other than mere figures." (1871).

"Do you believe that if France, instead of being governed, in short, by the mob, were in the power of the mandarins, we would be in this mess? If, instead of having wanted to enlighten the lower classes, we had been concerned with educating the upper ones?" (Croisset, Wednesday, August 3rd, 1870).

ond, black psychology. For example, when Flaubert declared that he called "anyone who thought basely bourgeois," he was defining the bourgeois in psychological and idealistic terms, that is, in the perspective of the ideology which he pretended to reject. As a result, he rendered a signal service to the bourgeoisie. He led back to the fold the rebellious and the maladjusted, who might have gone over to the proletariat, by convincing them that one could cast off the bourgeois in himself by a simple inner discipline. All they had to do was to practice high thinking in private and they could continue to enjoy their goods and prerogatives with a peaceful conscience. They could still live in bourgeois fashion, and enjoy their incomes in bourgeois fashion, and frequent bourgeois drawing-rooms, but that would all be nothing but appearance. They had raised themselves above their kind by the nobility of their feelings. By the same token he taught his confrères the trick which could allow them, at any rate, to maintain a good conscience; for magnanimity finds its most fitting practice in the practice of the arts.

The solitude of the artist was doubly a fake: it covered up not only a real relationship with the great public but also the restoration of an audience of specialists. Since the government of men and goods was abandoned to the bourgeoisie, the spiritual was once again separated from the temporal. A sort of priesthood once again sprang up. Stendhal's public was Balzac, Baudelaire's was Barbey d'Aurevilly; and Baudelaire, in turn, made himself the public of Poe. These literary salons took on a vague collegiate atmosphere; one "talked literature" in a hushed voice, with an infinite respect; one debated whether the musician derived more aesthetic joy from his music than the writer from his books. Art again became sacred to the extent that it turned aside from life. It even set up for itself a sort of communion of saints; one joined hands across the centuries with Cervantes, Rabelais, and Dante. One identified himself with this monastic society. The priesthood, instead of being a concrete and, so to speak, geographical organism, became a hereditary institution, a club, all of whose members were dead except one, the last in point of time, who represented the others upon earth and who epitomized the whole college.

These new believers, who had their saints in the past, also had their future life. The divorce of the temporal and spiritual led to a deep modification of the idea of glory. From the time of Racine on, it had been not so much the revenge of the misunderstood writer as the natural prolongation of success in an immutable society. In the nineteenth century it functioned as a mechanism of overcompensation. "I shall be understood in 1880," "I shall win my trial on appeal;" these famous words prove that the writer had not lost the desire to practise a direct and universal action within the framework of an integrated collectivity. But as this action was not possible in the present, one projected into an indefinite future the compensatory myth of a reconciliation between the writer and his public. Moreover, all this remained quite vague; none of these lovers of glory asked himself in what sort of society he would be able to find his recompense. They merely took pleasure in dreaming that their great-nephews would profit from an internal betterment for having come at a later time into an older world. That was the way

Baudelaire, who didn't worry about contradictions, often dressed his wounded pride, by considering his posthumous renown, although he held that society had entered a period of decadence which would end only with the disappearance of the human race.

Thus, for the present, the writer relied on an audience of specialists; as for the past, he concluded a mystic pact with the great dead; as to the future, he made use of the myth of glory. He neglected nothing in wrenching himself free from his class. He was up in the air, a stranger to his century, out of his element, damned. All this playacting had but one goal: to integrate himself into a symbolic society which would be like an image of the aristocracy of the old régime. Psychoanalysis is familiar with these processes of identification of which artistic thinking offers numerous examples: the sick person who needs the key of the asylum in order to escape and finally comes to believe that he himself is the key. Thus, the writer, who needed the favor of the great to unclass himself, ended by taking himself for the incarnation of the whole nobility, and as the latter was characterized by its parasitism it was the ostentation of parasitism which he chose for his style of living. He made himself the martyr of pure consumption. As we have pointed out, he saw no objection to using the goods of the bourgeoisie, but on condition that he was to spend them, that is, transform them into unproductive and useless objects. He burned them, so to speak, because fire purifies everything. Moreover, as he was not always rich, and as he had to live well, he composed a strange life for himself, both extravagant and needy, in which a calculated improvidence symbolized the

127

mad liberality which was denied him. Outside of art, he found nobility in only three kinds of occupation. First, in love, because it is a useless passion and because women, as Nietzsche said, are the most dangerous game. Also in travel, because the traveler is a perpetual witness who passes from one society to another without ever remaining in any because as a *foreign* consumer in an industrious collectivity, he is the very image of parasitism. Sometimes, in war too, because it is an immense consumption of men and goods.

The contempt with which trade was regarded in aristocratic and warlike societies was again met with in the writer. He was not satisfied with being useless, like the courtiers of the Old Régime; he wanted to be able to trample on utilitarian work, to smash it, burn it, damage it; he wanted to imitate the unconstraint of the lords who had their hunting parties ride across the ripe wheat. He cultivated in himself those destructive impulses of which Baudelaire has spoken in *The Glass-maker*. A little later he was to have a particular liking for instruments which were defective, worthless or no longer in use, half retrieved by nature, and which were like caricatures of instrumentality. It was not a rare thing for him to consider his own life as a tool to be destroyed. In any event, he risked it and played to lose: alcohol, drugs, everything served his purpose. The height of uselessness, of course, was beauty. From "art for art's sake" to symbolism, including realism and the Parnassians, all schools agreed that art was the highest form of pure consumption. It taught nothing, it reflected no ideology, and above all, it refrained from moralizing. Long before Gide wrote it,

Flaubert, Gautier, the Goncourts, Renard, and Maupassant had in their own way said that "it is with good sentiments that one produces bad literature."

For some, literature was subjectivity carried to the absolute, a bonfire in which the black vines of their sufferings and vices writhed and twisted. Lying at the bottom of a world as in a dungeon, they passed beyond it and dispelled it by their dissatisfaction, which revealed other worlds to them. It seemed to them that their heart was different enough so that the picture of it which they drew might be resolutely barren. Others set themselves up as the impartial witnesses of their age, but nobody noticed that they were testifying. They raised testimony and witness to the absolute; they offered to the empty sky the tableau of the society about them. Circumvented, transposed, unified, and caught in the trap of an artistic style, the events of the universe were neutralized and, so to speak, put in parentheses; realism was an "epoché." Here impossible truth joined hands with inhuman Beauty "beautiful as a marble dream." Neither the author, insofar as he wrote, nor the reader, insofar as he read, any longer belonged to this world: they were transformed into pure beholding; they considered man from without; they strove to see him from the point of view of God, or, if you like, of the absolute void. But after all, I can still recognize myself in the purest lyricist's description of his particularities. And if the experimental novel imitated science, was it not utilizable as science was? Could it not likewise have its social *applications?*

The extremists wished, for fear of being serviceable, that their works should not even enlighten the reader about his own heart; they refused to transmit their experience. In the last analysis the work would be entirely gratuitous only if it were entirely inhuman. The logical conclusion of all this was the hope of an absolute creation, a quintessence of luxury and prodigality, not utilizable in this world because it *was not of the world* and because it recalled nothing in it. Imagination was conceived as an unconditioned faculty of *denying* the real and the *objet d'art* was set up on the collapsing of the universe. There was the heightened artificialism of Des Esseintes, the systematic deranging of all the senses, and finally the concerted destruction of language. There was also silence: that icy silence, the work of Mallarmé—or the silence of M. Teste for whom all communication was impure.

The extreme point of this brilliant and mortal literature was nothingness. Its extreme point and its deeper essence. There was nothing positive in the new spirituality. It was a pure and simple negation of the temporal. In the Middle Ages it was the temporal which was the Inessential in relation to spirituality; in the nineteenth century the opposite occurred: the Temporal was primary and the spiritual was the inessential parasite which gnawed away at it and tried to destroy it. It was a question of denying the world or consuming it. Of denying it by consuming it. Flaubert wrote to disentangle himself from men and things. His sentence surrounds the object, seizes it, immobilizes it and breaks its back, changes into stone and petrifies the object as well. It is blind and deaf, without arteries; not a breath of life. A deep silence separates it from the sentence which follows; it falls into the void, eternally, and drags its prey along in this infinite fall. Once described, any reality is stricken from the inventory; one moves on to the next. Realism was nothing else but this great gloomy chase. It was a matter of setting one's mind at rest before anything else. Wherever one went, the grass stopped growing. The determinism of the naturalistic novel crushed out life and replaced human actions by one-way mechanisms. It had virtually but one subject: the slow disintegration of a man, an enterprise, a family, or a society. It was necessary to return to zero. One took nature in a state of productive disequilibrium and one wiped out this disequilibrium; one returned to an equilibrium of death by annulling the forces with which he was confronted. When, by chance, he shows us the success of an ambitious man, it is only appearance; Bel Ami does not take the strongholds of the bourgeoisie by assault; he is a gauge whose rise merely testifies to the collapse of a society. And when symbolism discovered the close relationship between beauty and death, it was merely making explicit the theme of the whole literature of a half century. The beauty of the past, because it is gone; the beauty of young people dying and of flowers which fade; the beauty of all erosions and all ruins; the supreme dignity of consumption, of the disease which consumes, of the love which devours, of the art which kills; death is everywhere, before us, behind us, even in the sun and the perfumes of the earth. The art of Barrès is a meditation on death: a thing is beautiful only when it is "consumable," that is, it dies when one has enjoyed it.

The temporal structure which was particularly appropriate for these princely games was the moment. Because it passes and because in itself it is the image of eternity, it is the negation of human time, that three dimensional time of work and history. A great deal of time is needed to build; a moment is enough to hurl everything to the ground. When one considers the work of Gide in this perspective, one cannot help seeing in it an ethics strictly reserved for the writer-consumer. What is his gratuitous act if not the culmination of a century of bourgeois comedy and the imperative of the author-gentleman: Philoctète gives away his bow, the millionaire squanders his banknotes, Bernard steals, Lafcadio kills and Ménalque sells his belongings.

This destructive movement was to go to its logical consequence: "The simplest surrealist act," Breton was to write twenty years later, "consists of going down into the street, revolver in hand, and firing into the crowd at random as long as you can." It was the last term of a long dialectical process. In the eighteenth century literature had been a negativity; in the reign of the bourgeoisie it passed on to a state of absolute and hypostasized Negation. It became a multicolored and glittering process of annihilation. "Surrealism is not interested in paying much attention . . . to anything whose end is not the annihilation of being and its transformation into an internal and blind brilliance which is no more the soul of ice than it is of fire," writes Breton once again. In the end there is nothing left for literature to do but to contest itself. That is what it did in the name of surrealism. For seventy years writers had been working to consume the world; after 1918 one wrote in order to consume literature: one squandered literary traditions, hashed together words, threw them against each other to make them shatter. Literature as Negation became Anti-literature; never had it been more *literary*: the circle was completed.

During the same time, the writer, in order to imitate the lighthearted squandering of an aristocracy of birth, had no greater concern than that of establishing his irresponsibility. He began by setting up the rights of genius which replaced the divine right of the authoritarian monarchy. Since Beauty was luxury carried to the extreme, since it was a pyre with cold flames which lit up and and consumed everything, since it was fed by all forms of deterioration and destruction, in particular suffering and death, the artist, who was its priest, had the right to demand in its name and to provoke, if need be, the unhappiness of those close to him. As for him, he had been burning for a long time; he was in ashes; other victims were needed to feed the flames. Women in particular: they would make him suffer and he would pay them back with interest. He wanted to be able to bring bad luck to everyone around him. And if there were no means of setting off catastrophes, he would accept offerings. Admirers, male and female, were there so that he might set fire to their hearts or spend their money without gratitude or remorse. Maurice Sachs reports that his maternal grandfather, who had a fanatical admiration for Anatole France, spent a fortune furnishing the Villa Saïd. When he died, Anatole France uttered this funeral eulogy: "Too bad! He was decorative." By taking money from the bourgeois, the writer was practising his priesthood, since he was diverting a part of their wealth in order to send it up in smoke. And by the same token

133

he placed himself above all responsibilities: whom could he be responsible to? And in the name of what? If his work aimed at constructing, he could be asked to give an accounting. But since it declared itself to be pure destruction, it escaped judgment.

At the end of the century all this remained somewhat confused and contradictory. But when literature, with surrealism, made itself a provocation to murder, one saw the writer, by a paradoxical but logical sequence, explicitly setting up the principle of his total irresponsibility. To tell the truth, he did not make his reasons clear; he took refuge in the bushes of automatic writing. But the motives are evident: a parasitic aristocracy of pure consumption, whose function was to keep burning the goods of an industrious and productive society, could not come under the jurisdiction of the collectivity he was destroying. And as this systematic destruction never went any further than *scandal*, this amounted in the last analysis, to saying that the primary duty of the writer was to provoke scandal and that his inalienable right was to escape its consequences.

The bourgeoisie let him carry on; it smiled at these monkey shines. What did it matter if the writer scorned it? This scorn wouldn't lead to anything since the bourgeoisie was his only public. It was the only one to whom he spoke about it; it was a secret between them; in a way, it was the bond which united them. And even if he won the popular audience, what likelihood was there of stirring up the discontent of the masses by showing that bourgeois thinking was contemptible? There was not the slightest chance that a doctrine of absolute consumption could fool the working classes. Besides, the bourgeoisie knew very well that the writer secretly took its part: he needed it for his aesthetic of opposition and resentment; it provided him with the goods he consumed; he wanted to preserve the social order so that he could feel that as a stranger there he was a permanent fixture. In short, he was a rebel, not a revolutionary.

As for rebels, they were right in the bourgeoisie's line. In a sense, it even became their accomplice; it was better to keep the forces of negation within a vain aestheticism, a rebellion without effect; if they were free, they might have interested themselves on behalf of the oppressed classes. And then, bourgeois readers understood, in their way, what the writer called the *gratuity* of his work; for the latter this was the very essence of spirituality and the heroic manifestation of his break with the temporal; for the former a gratuitous work was fundamentally inoffensive; it was an amusement. They doubtless preferred the literature of Bordeaux and Bourget but they did not think that it was bad if there were useless books; they distracted the mind from serious preoccupations; they provided it with the recreation it needed for its general well-being. Thus, even while recognizing that the work of art could serve no purpose, the bourgeois public still found means of utilizing it.

The writer's success was built upon this misunderstanding; as he rejoiced in being misunderstood, it was normal for his readers to be mistaken. Since literature had become in his hands an abstract negation which fed on itself, he must have expected them to smile at his most cutting insults and say "it's only literature;" and since it

135

was a pure contestation of the spirit of seriousness, he must have been pleased that they refused on principle to take him seriously. Thus, they found themselves, even though it was with scandal and without quite realizing it, in the most "nihilistic" works of the age. The reason was that even though the writer might have put all his efforts into concealing his readers from himself, he could never completely escape their insidious influence. A shame-faced bourgeois, writing for bourgeois without admitting it to himself, he was able to launch the maddest ideas; the ideas were often only bubbles which popped up on the surface of his mind. But his technique betrayed him because he did not watch over it with the same zeal. It expressed a deeper and truer choice, an obscure metaphysic, a genuine relationship with contemporary society. Whatever the cynicism and the bitterness of the chosen subject, nineteenth-century narrative technique offered the French public a reassuring image of the bourgeoisie. Our authors, to be sure, inherited it, but they were responsible for having perfected it.

Its appearance, which dates from the end of the Middle Ages, coincided with the first reflective meditation by which the novelist became conscious of his art. At first he told his story without putting himself on the stage or meditating on his function because the subjects of his tales were almost always of folk or, at any rate, collective origin, and he limited himself to making use of them. The social character of the matter he worked with as well as the fact that it existed before he came to be concerned with it conferred upon him the role of intermediary and was enough to justify him; he was the man who knew the most charming stories and who, instead of telling them orally, set them down in writing. He invented little; he gave them style; he was the historian of the imaginary. When he himself started contriving the fiction which he published, he found himself. He discovered simultaneously his almost guilty solitude and unjustifiable gratuity, the subjectivity of literary creation. In order to mask them from the eyes of others and from his own as well, in order to establish his right to tell these stories, he wanted to give his inventions the appearance of truth. Lacking the power to preserve the almost material opacity which characterized them when they emanated from the collective imagination, he pretended that at least they did not originate with him, and he managed to give them out as memories. To do that he had represented himself in his works by means of a narrator of oral tradition and at the same time he inserted into them a fictitious audience which represented his real public, such as the characters in the *Decameron* whom their temporary exile puts curiously in the position of learned people and who in turn take up the role of narrator, audience, and critic. Thus, after the age of objective and metaphysical realism, when the words of the tale were taken for the very things which they named and when its substance was the universe, there came that of literary idealism in which the word has existence only in someone's mouth or on someone's pen and refers back in essence to a speaker to whose presence it bears witness, where the substance of the tales is the subjectivity which perceives and thinks the universe, and where the novelist, instead of putting the reader directly into contact with the object, has become conscious of his role of mediator and embodies the mediation in a fictitious recital.

Since that time the chief characteristic of the story which one gives to the public has been that of being already thought, that is, achieved, set in order, pruned, and clarified; or rather, of yielding itself only through the thoughts which one retrospectively forms about it. That is why the tense of the novel is almost always the past, whereas that of the epic, which is of collective origin, is frequently the present.

Passing from Boccaccio to Cervantes and then to the French novels of the seventeenth and eighteenth centuries, the proceedings grow complicated and become episodic because the novel picks up along the way and incorporates the satire, the fable, and the character sketch.[1] The novelist appears in the first chapter; he announces, he questions his readers, admonishes them, and assures them of the truth of his story. I shall call this "primary subjectivity." Then, secondary characters intervene along the way, characters whom the narrator has met and who interrupt the course of the plot to tell the story of their own misfortunes. These are the "secondary subjectivities" supported and restored by the primary subjectivity. Thus, certain stories are re-thought and intellectualized to the second degree.[2] The readers never experience the direct

1. In *The Devil on Two Sticks*, for example, Le Sage *novelizes* the characters of La Bruyere and the maxims of La Rochefoucauld; that is, he binds them together by the slender thread of a plot.

2. The procedure of writing the novel in the form of letters is only a variation of what I have just indicated. The letter is the subjective recital of an event; it refers back to the one who wrote it and who becomes both actor and witnessing subjectivity. As to the event itself, although it is recent, it is already re-thought and explained: the letter always supposes a lag between the fact (which belongs to a recent past) and its recital, which is given subsequently and in a moment of leisure.

138

onrush of the event; if the narrator has been surprised by it at the moment of its occurrence, he does not *communicate* his surprise to them; he simply *informs* them of it. As to the novelist, since he is convinced that the only reality of the word lies in its being said, since he lives in a polite century in which there still exists an art of conversation, he introduces conversationalists into his book in order to justify the words which are read there; but since it is by words that he represents the characters whose function is to talk, he does not escape the vicious circle.[1]

Of course, the authors of the nineteenth century brought their efforts to bear on the narration of the event. They tried to restore part of its freshness and violence, but for the most part they again took up the idealistic technique and adapted it to their needs. Authors as dissimilar as Barbey d'Aurevilly and Fromentin make use of it constantly. In *Dominique*, for example, one finds a primary subjectivity which manipulates the levels of a secondary subjectivity and it is the latter which makes the tale. The procedure is nowhere more manifest than in Maupassant. The structure of his short stories is almost invariable; we are first presented with the audience, a brilliant and worldly society which has assembled in a drawing-room after dinner. It is night-time, which dispels fatigue and passion. The oppressed are asleep, as are the rebellious; the world is enshrouded; the story unfolds. In a bubble of light surrounded by nothing there remains this élite which stays awake, completely occupied with its

---

1. This is the reverse of the vicious circle of the surrealists who try to destroy painting by painting. In this case one wants to have literature's letters of credit given by literature.

ceremonies. If there are intrigues or love or hate among its members, we are not told of them, and desire and anger are likewise stilled; these men and women are occupied in *preserving* their culture and manners and in *recognizing* each other by the rites of politeness. They represent order in its most exquisite form; the calm of night, the silence of the passions, everything concurs in symbolizing the stable bourgeoisie of the end of the century which thinks that nothing more will happen and which believes in the eternity of capitalist organization. Thereupon, the narrator is introduced. He is a middle-aged man who has "seen much, read much, and retained much," a professional man of experience, a doctor, a military man, an artist, or a Don Juan. He has reached the time of life when, according to a respectful and comfortable myth, man is freed from the passions and considers with an indulgent lucidity those he has experienced. His heart is calm, like the night. He tells his story with detachment. If it has caused him suffering, he has made honey from this suffering. He looks back upon it and considers it as it really was, that is, *sub specie aeternitatis*. There was difficulty to be sure, but this difficulty ended long ago; the actors are dead or married or comforted. Thus, the adventure was a brief disturbance which is over with. It is told from the viewpoint of experience and wisdom; it is listened to from the viewpoint of order. Order triumphs; order is everywhere; it contemplates an old disorder as if the still waters of a summer day have preserved the memory of the ripples which have run through it. Moreover, had there even been this disturbance? The evocation of an abrupt change would frighten this bourgeois sociey. Neither the general nor the doctor confides his recollections in the raw state; they are experiences from which they have extracted the quintessence, and they warn us, from the moment they start talking, that their tale has a moral. Besides, the story is explanatory; it aims at producing a psychological law on the basis of this example. A law, or, as Hegel says, the calm image of change. And the change itself, that is, the individual aspect of the anecdote, is it not an appearance? To the extent that one explains it, one reduces the entire effect to the entire cause, the unforeseen to the expected and the new to the old. The narrator brings the same workmanship to bear upon the human event as, according to Myerson, the nineteenth-century scientist brought to bear upon the scientific fact. He reduces the diverse to the identical. And if, from time to time, he maliciously desires to maintain a slightly disquieting tone in his story, he dispenses the irreducibility of the change most carefully, as in those fantastic tales in which, behind the inexplicable, the author allows us to suspect a whole causal order which will restore rationality in the universe. Thus, for the novelist who is a product of this stabilized society change is a non-being, as it is for Parmenides, as Evil is for Claudel. Moreover, even should it exist, it would never be anything else than an individual calamity in a maladjusted soul.

It is not a question of studying the relative movements of partial systems within a system in motion — society, the universe — but of considering from the viewpoint of absolute rest the absolute movement of a relatively isolated partial system. That is, one sets up absolute landmarks in order to determine it, and consequently one knows it in its absolute truth. In an ordered society which meditates upon its eternity and celebrates it with rites, a man evokes the phantom of a past diseasiness, dispels it with a wave of his magic wand and order, makes it glitter, embellishes it with old-fashioned graces, and at the moment when he is about to cause unsubstitutes for it the eternal hierarchy of causes and laws. In this magician who frees himself from history and life by understanding them and who is raised above his audience by his knowledge and experience we recognize the loftly aristocrat whom we spoke about earlier.[1]

If we have spoken at some length about Maupassant's narrative procedure it is because it constituted the basic technique for all the French novelists of his own generation, of the succeeding one, and of all the generations since. The internal narrator is always present. He may reduce himself to an abstraction; often he is not even explicitly designated; but, at any rate, it is through his subjectivity that we perceive the event. When he does not appear at all, it is not that he has been suppressed like a useless device; it is that he has become the *alter ego* of the author. The latter, with his blank sheet of paper in front of him, sees his imagination transmuted into experiences. He no longer writes in his own name but at the dictation of a mature and sober man who has witnessed the circumstances which are being related.

1. When Maupassant writes *Le Horla,* that is, when he speaks of the madness which threatens him, the tone changes. It is because at last something — something horrible — is going to happen. The man is overwhelmed, crushed; he no longer understands; he wants to drag the reader along with him into his terror. But the twig is bent; lacking a technique adapted to madness, death, and history, he fails to move the reader.

Daudet, for example, obviously had the mind of a drawing-room raconteur who infuses into his style the twists and friendly casualness of worldly conversation, who exclaims, grows ironical, questions, and challenges his audience: "Ah! how disappointed Tartarin was! And do you know why? You won't guess in a million years!" Even realistic writers who wished to be the objective historians of their time preserved the abstract scheme of the method; that is, in all their novels there is a common milieu, a common plot, which is not the individual and historical subjectivity of the novelist but the ideal and universal one of the man of experience. First of all, the tale is laid in the past: the ceremonial past, in order to put some distance between the events and the audience; the subjective past, equivalent to the memory of the story-teller; the social past, since the plot does not belong to that history without conclusion which is in the making but to history already made.

If it is true, as Janet claims, that memory is distinguished from the somnambulistic resurrection of the past in that the latter reproduces the event, whereas the former, indefinitely compressible, can be told in a phrase or a volume, according to need, it can well be said that novels of this kind, with their abrupt contractions of time followed by long expansions, are precisely memories. Sometimes the novelist lingers to describe a decisive moment; at other times he leaps across several years: "Three years flowed by, three years of gloomy suffering..." He permits himself to shed light on his characters' present by means of their future: "They did not think at the time that this brief encounter was to have fatal consequences. . ." And from his point of view he is not wrong, since this present and future are both past, since the time of memory has lost its irreversibility and one can cross it backward and forward.

Besides, the memories which he gives us, already worked upon, thought over, and appraised, offer us an immediately assimilable teaching; the feelings and actions are often presented to us as typical examples of the laws of the heart: "Daniel, like all young people . . .," "Eve was quite feminine in that she . . .," "Mercier had the nasty habit, common among civil-service clerks . . ." And as these laws cannot be deduced *a priori* nor grasped by intuition nor founded on experimentation which is scientific and capable of being universally reproduced, they refer the reader back to a subjectivity which has produced these recipes from the circumstances of an active life. In this sense it can be said that most of the French novels of the Third Republic aspired, whatever the age of their real author and much more so if the author was very young, to the honor of having been written by quinquagenarians.

During this whole period, which extends over several generations, the plot is related from the point of view of the absolute, that is, of order. It is a local change in a system at rest; neither the author nor the reader runs any risk; there is no surprise to be feared; the event is a thing of the past; it has been catalogued and understood. In a stable society which is not yet conscious of the dangers which threaten it, which has a morality at its disposal, a scale of values, and a system of explanations to integrate its local changes, which is convinced that it is beyond

144

historicity and that nothing important will ever happen any more, in a bourgeois France tilled to the last acre, laid out like a checkerboard by its secular walls, congealed in its industrial methods, and resting on the glory of its Revolution, no other fictional technique could be possible. New methods that some writers attempted to introduce were successful only as curiosities or were not followed up. Neither writers, readers, the structure of the collectivity, nor its myths had any need of them.[1]

Thus, whereas literature ordinarily represents an integrating and militant function in society, bourgeois society at the end of the nineteenth century offers the unprecedented spectacle of an industrious society, grouped around the banner of production, from which there issues a literature which, far from reflecting it, never speaks to it about what interests it, runs counter to its ideology, identifies the Beautiful with the unproductive, refuses to

---

1. Among these procedures I shall first cite the curious recourse to the style of the theatre that one finds at the end of the last century and the beginning of this one in Gyp, Lavedan, Abel Hermant, etc. The novel was written in dialogue form. The gestures of the characters and their actions were indicated in italics and parenthetically. It was evidently a matter of making the reader contemporaneous with the action as the spectator is during the performance. This procedure certainly manifests the predominance of dramatic art in polite society around 1900. In its way it also sought to escape the myth of primary subjectivity. But the fact that it was abandoned shows sufficiently that it did not solve the problem. First, it is a sign of weakness to ask for help from a neighboring art, a proof that one lacks resources in the very domain of the art he practices. Then, the author did not thereby keep from entering into the consciousness of his characters and having the reader enter with him. He simply divulged the intimate contents of the consciousness in parentheses and italics, with the style and typographical procedures that are generally used for stage directions. In effect, it was an attempt without a future. The authors who used it had a vague feeling that new life could be put into the novel by writing it in the present. But they had not yet understood that it was not possible if one did not first give up the *explanatory attitude*.

More serious was the attempt to introduce the interior monologue of Schnitz-

allow itself to be integrated, and does not even wish to be read.

The authors are not to be blamed; they did what they could; among them are some of our greatest and purest writers. And besides, as every kind of human behavior discloses to us an aspect of the universe, their attitude has enriched us despite themselves by revealing gratuity as one of the infinite dimensions of the world and as a possible goal of human activity. And as they were artists, their work covered up a desperate appeal to the freedom of the reader they pretended to despise. It pushed contestation to the limit, even to the point of contesting itself; it gives us a glimpse of a black silence beyond the massacre of words, and, beyond the spirit of seriousness, the bare and empty sky of equivalences; it invites us to emerge into nothingness by destruction of all myths and all

ler (I am not speaking here of that of Joyce which has quite different metaphysical principles. Larbaud, who, I know, harks back to Joyce, seems to me much rather to draw his inspiration from *Les Lauriers sont coupés* and from *Mademoiselle Else*). In short, it was a matter of pushing the hypothesis of a primary subjectivity to the limit and of passing on to realism by leading idealism up to the absolute.

The reality which one shows to the reader without intermediary is no longer the thing itself — the tree, the ashtray — but the consciousness which sees the thing; the "real" is no longer only a representation, but rather the representation becomes an absolute reality since it is given to us as an immediate datum. The inconvenient aspect of this procedure is that it encloses us in an individual subjectivity and that it thereby lacks the intermonadic universe; besides, it dilutes the event and the action in the perception of one and then the other. Now, the common characteristic of the fact and the action is that they escape subjective representation which grasps their results but not their living movement. In short, it is only with a certain amount of faking that one reduces the stream of consciousness to a succession of words, even deformed ones. If the word is given as an intermediary *signifying* a reality which in essence transcends language, nothing could be better; it withdraws itself, is forgotten, and discharges consciousness upon the object.

But if it presents itself as the *psychic reality*, if the author, by writing,

scales of value; it discloses to us in man a close and secret relationship with the nothing, instead of the intimate relationship with the divine transcendence. It is the literature of adolescence, of that age when the young man, useless and without responsibility, still supported and fed by his parents, wastes his family's money, passes judgment on his father, and takes part in the demolition of the serious universe which protected his childhood. If one bears in mind that the festival, as Caillois has well shown, is one of those negative moments when the collectivity consumes the goods it has accumulated, violates the laws of its moral code, spends for the pleasure of spending, and destroys for the pleasure of destroying, it will be seen that literature in the nineteenth century was, on the margin of the industrious society which had the *mystique* of saving, a great sumptuous and funereal festival, an invitation

---

claims to give us an ambiguous reality which is a sign, objective in essence — that is, insofar as it relates to something outside itself — and a thing, formal in essence — that is, as an immediate psychic datum — then he can be accused of not having participated and of disregarding the rhetorical law which might be formulated as follows: in literature, where one uses signs, it is not necessary to use *only* signs; and if the *reality* which one wants to signify is *one word*, it must be given to the reader by other words. He can be charged, besides, with having forgotten that the greatest riches of the psychic life are *silent*. We know what has happened to the internal monologue; having become *rhetoric*, that is, a poetic transposition of the inner life — silent as well as verbal — it has today become one method *among others* of the novelist. Too idealistic to be true, too realistic to be complete. it is the crown of the subjectivistic technique. It is within and by means of this technique that the literature of to-day has become conscious of itself, that is, that literature is a double surpassing, toward the objective and toward the rhetorical, of the technique of the internal monologue. But for that it is necessary that the historical circumstance change.

It is evident that the writer continues to-day to write in the past tense. It is not by changing the tense of the verb but by revolutionizing the techniques of the story that he will succeed in making the reader contemporary with the story.

to burn in a splendid immorality, in the fire of the passions, even unto death. When I come to say later on that it found its belated fulfillment and its end in Trotskyising surrealism, one will better understand the function it assumes in a too closed society: it was a safety value. After all, it's not so far from the perpetual holiday to the permanent revolution.

However, the nineteenth century was the time of the writer's transgression and fall. Had he accepted unclassing from below and had he given his art a content, he would have carried on with other means and on another plane the undertaking of his predecessors. He might have helped literature pass from negativity and abstraction to concrete construction; without losing the autonomy which the eighteenth century had won for it and which there was no longer any question of taking away from it, it might have again integrated itself into society; by clarifying and supporting the claims of the proletariat, he would have attained the essence of the art of writing and would have understood that there is a coincidence not only between formal freedom of thought and political democracy, but also between the material obligation of choosing man as a perpetual subject of meditation and social democracy. His style would have regained an inner tension because he would have been addressing a split public. By trying to awaken the consciousness of the working class while giving evidence to the bourgeois of their own iniquity, his works would have reflected the entire world. He would have learned to distinguish generosity, the original source of the work of art, the unconditioned appeal to the reader, from prodigality, its caricature; he would have abandoned the analytical and psychological interpretation of "human nature" for the synthetic appreciation of *conditions*. Doubtless it was difficult, perhaps impossible; but he went about it the wrong way. It was not necessary for him to get on his high horse in a vain effort to escape all class determination, nor to "brood over" the proletariat, but on the contrary to think of himself as a bourgeois who had broken loose from his class and who was united with the oppressed masses by a solidarity of interest.

The sumptuousness of the means of expression which he discovered should not make us forget that he betrayed literature. But his responsibility goes even further; if the authors had found an audience in the oppressed classes, perhaps the divergence of their points of view and the diversity of their writings would have helped produce in the masses what someone has very happily called a *movement* of ideas, that is, an open, contradictory, and dialectical ideology. Without doubt, Marxism would have triumphed, but it would have been colored with a thousand nuances; it would have had to absorb rival doctrines, digest them, and remain open. We know what happened; two revolutionary ideologies instead of a hundred: before 1870, the Prudhonians in the majority in the International, then crushed by the defeat of the Commune; Marxism triumphing over its adversary not by the power of the Hegelian negativity which preserves while it surpasses, but because external forces pure and simple suppressed one of the forms of the antinomy. It would take a long time to tell all that this triumph without glory has cost Marxism; for want of contradiction, it has lost life. Had it been the better, constantly combatted, transforming itself in order to win, stealing its enemies' arms, it might have been identified with mind; alone, it became the Church, while the gentlemen-writers, a thousand miles away, made themselves guardians of an abstract spirituality.

Will anyone doubt that I am aware how incomplete and debatable these analyses are? Exceptions abound, and I know them, but it would take a big book to go into them. I have touched only the high spots. But above all, one should understand the spirit in which I have undertaken this work. If one were to see in it an attempt, even superficial, at sociological explanation, it would lose all significance. Just as for Spinoza, the idea of a line segment rotating about one of its extremities remains abstract and false if one considers it outside of the synthetic, concrete, and bounded idea of circumference which contains, completes, and justifies it, likewise here, the considerations remain arbitrary if they are not replaced in the perspective of a work of art, that is, of a free and unconditioned appeal to a freedom. One cannot write without a public and without a myth — without a *certain* public which historical circumstances have made, without a *certain* myth of literature which depends to a very great extent upon the demand of this public. In a word, the author is in a situation, like all other men. But his writings, like every human project, simultaneously enclose, specify, and surpass this situation, even explain it and set it up, just as the idea of a circle explains and sets up that of the rotation of a segment.

*Being situated* is an essential and necessary characteristic of freedom. To describe the situation is not to cast aspersion on the freedom. The Jansenist ideology, the law of the three unities, and the rules of French prosody are not art; in regard to art they are even pure nothingness, since they can by no means produce, by a simple combination, a good tragedy, a good scene, or even a good line. But the art of Racine had to be invented *on the basis* of these; not by conforming to them, as has been rather foolishly said, and by deriving exquisite difficulties and necessary constraints from them, but rather by re-inventing them, by conferring a new and peculiarly Racinian function upon the division into acts, the cesura, rhyme, and the ethics of Port Royale, so that it is impossible to decide whether he poured his subject into a mould which his age imposed upon him or whether he really elected this *technique* because his subject required it. To understand what *Phèdre* could not be, it is necessary to appeal to all anthropology. To understand what it *is*, it is necessary only to read or listen, that is, to make oneself a pure freedom and to give one's confidence generously to a generosity. The examples we have chosen have served only to *situate* the freedom of the writer in different ages, to illuminate by the limits of the demands made upon him the limits of his appeal, to show by the idea of his role which the public fashions for itself the necessary boundaries of the idea which he invents of literature. And if it is true that the essence of the literary work is freedom totally disclosing and willing itself as an appeal to the freedom of other men, it is also true that the different forms of oppression, by hiding from men the fact that they were free, have screened all or part of this essence from authors. Thus, the opinions which they have formed about their profession are necessarily truncated. There is always some truth tucked away in them, but this partial and isolated truth becomes an error if one stops there, and the social movement permits us to conceive the fluctuations of the literary idea, although each particular work surpasses, in a certain way, all conceptions which one can have of art, because it is always, in a certain sense, unconditioned, because it comes out of nothingness and holds the world in suspense in nothingness. In addition, as our descriptions have permitted us to catch a glimpse of a sort of dialectic of the idea of literature, we can, without in the least pretending to give a history of belles-lettres, restore the movement of this dialectic in the last few centuries in order to discover at the end, be it as an ideal, the pure essence of the literary work and, conjointly, the type of public — that is, of society — which it requires.

I say that the literature of a given age is alienated when it has not arrived at the explicit consciousness of its autonomy and when it submits to temporal powers or to an ideology, in short, when it considers itself as a means and not as an unconditioned end. There is no doubt that literary works, in their particularity, surpass this servitude and that each one contains an unconditioned exigence, but only by implication. I say that a literature is abstract when it has not yet acquired the full view of its essence, when it has merely set up the principle of its formal autonomy and when it considers the subject of the work as indifferent. From this point of view the twelfth century offers us the image of a concrete and alienated literature. Concrete, because content and form are blended; one learns to write only to write about God; the book is the mirror of the world insofar as the world is His work; it is an inessential creation on the margin of a major Creation; it is praise, psalm, offering, a pure reflection. By the same token literature falls into alienation; that is, since it is, in any case, the reflectiveness of the social body, since it remains in the state of non-reflective reflectiveness, it mediatizes the Catholic universe; but for the clerk it remains the immediate; it retrieves the world, but by losing itself. But as the reflective idea must necessarily reflect *itself* on pain of annihilating itself with the whole reflected universe, the three examples which we have studied showed a movement of the retrieving of literature by itself, that is, its transition from the state of unreflective and immediate reflection to that of reflective mediation. At first concrete and alienated, it liberates itself by negativity and passes to abstraction; more exactly, it passes in the eighteenth century to abstract negativity before becoming in the late nineteenth and early twentieth century absolute negation. At the end of this evolution it has cut all its bonds with society; it no longer even has a public. "Every one knows," writes Paulhan, "that there are two literatures in our time, the bad, which is really unreadable (it is widely read) and the good, which is not read."

But even that is an advance; at the end of this lofty isolation, at the end of this scornful rejection of all efficacity there is the destruction of literature by itself; at first, the terrible "it's *only* literature;" then, that literary phenomenon which the same Paulhan calls terrorism, which is born at about the same time as the idea of parasitic gratuity, and as its antithesis, and which runs all through the nineteenth century, contracting as it goes a

153

thousand irrational marriages and which finally bursts forth shortly before the first war. Terrorism, or rather the terrorist complex, for it is a tangle of vipers. One might distinguish, first, so deep a disgust with the sign as such that it leads in all cases to preferring the thing signified to the word, the act to the statement, the word conceived as object to the word-signification, that is, in the last analysis, poetry to prose, spontaneous disorder to composition; second, an effort to make literature one expression among others of life, instead of sacrificing life to literature; and third, a crisis of the writer's moral conscience, that is the sad collapse of parasitism. Thus, without for a moment conceiving the idea of losing its formal autonomy, literature makes itself a negation of formalism and comes to raise the question of its essential content. To-day we are beyond terrorism and we can make use of its experience and the preceding analyses to set down the essential traits of a concrete and liberated literature.

We have said that, as a rule, the writer addressed all men. But immediately afterward we noted that he was read only by a few. As a result of the divergence between the real public and the ideal public, there arose the idea of abstract universality. That is, the author postulates the constant repetition in an indefinite future of the handful of readers which he has at present. Literary glory peculiarly resembles Nietzsche's eternal recurrence; it is a struggle against history; here, as there, recourse to the infinity of time seeks to compensate for the failure in space (for the author of the seventeenth century, a recurrence *ad infinitum* of the gentleman; for the one of the nineteenth century, an extension *ad infinitum* of the club of writers and the public of specialists). But as it is self-evident that the effect of the projection into the future of the real and present public is to perpetuate, at least in the representation of the writer, the exclusion of the majority of men, as, in addition, this imagining of an infinity of unborn readers is tantamount to extending the actual public by a public made up of merely possible men, the universality which glory aims at is partial and abstract. And as the choice of the public conditions, to a certain extent, the choice of subject, the literature which has set up glory as its goal and its governing idea must also remain abstract.

The term "concrete universality" must be understood, on the contrary, as the sum total of men living in a given society. If the writer's public could ever be extended to the point of embracing this totality, the result would not be that he would necessarily have to limit the reverberations of his work to the present time, but rather he would oppose to the abstract eternity of glory, which is an impossible and hollow dream of the absolute, a concrete and finite duration which he would determine by the very choice of his subjects, and which, far from uprooting him from history, would define his situation in social time. As a matter of fact, every human project outlines a certain future by its very motto: if I'm going to sow, I'm putting a whole year of waiting before me; if I get married, my venture suddenly causes my whole life to rise up before me; if I launch out into politics, I'm mortgaging a future which will extend beyond my death. The same with writing. Already, under the pretense of belaureled immortality, one discerns more modest and more concrete pretensions. The aim of *The Silence of the Sea* was to lead the French to reject the enemy's efforts to get them to collaborate. Its effectiveness and consequently its actual public could not extend beyond the time of the occupation. The books of Richard Wright will remain alive as long as the negro question is raised in the United States. Thus, there is no question as to the writer's renouncing the idea of survival; quite the contrary, he is the one who decides it; he will survive so long as he acts. Afterward, it's honorary membership, retirement. Today, for having wanted to escape from history, he begins his honorary membership the day after his death, sometimes even while he is alive.

Thus, the concrete public would be a tremendous feminine questioning, the waiting of a whole society which the writer would have to seduce and satisfy. But for that the public would have to be free to ask and the writer to answer. That means that in no case must the questions of one group or class cover up those of other milieus; otherwise, we would relapse into the abstract. In short, *actual* literature can only realize its full *essence* in a classless society. Only in this society could the writer be aware that there is no difference of any kind between his *subject* and his *public*. For the subject of literature has always been man in the world. However, as long as the virtual public remained like a dark sea around the sunny little beach of the real public, the writer risked confusing the interests and cares of man with those of a small and favored group. But, if the public were identified with the concrete universal, the writer would really have to write about the human totality. Not about the abstract man of all the ages and for a timeless reader, but about the whole man of his age and for his contemporaries. As a result, the literary antinomy of lyrical subjectivity and objective testimony would be left behind. Involved in the same adventure as his readers and situated like them in a society without cleavages, the writer, in speaking about them, would be speaking about himself, and in speaking about himself would be speaking about them. As no aristocratic pride would any longer force him to deny that he is in a situation, he would no longer seek to soar above his times and bear witness to it before eternity, but, as his situation would be universal, he would express the hopes and anger of all men, and would thereby express himself completely, that is, not as a metaphysical creature like the medieval clerk, nor as a psychological animal like our classical writers, nor even as a social entity, but as a totality emerging into the world from the void and containing within it all those structures in the indissoluble unity of the human condition; literature would really be anthropological, in the full sense of the term.

It is quite evident that in such a society there would be nothing which would even remotely recall the separation of the temporal and the spiritual. Indeed, we have seen that this division necessarily corresponds to an alienation of man and, therefore, of literature; our analyses have shown us that it always tends to oppose a public of professionals or, at least, of enlightened amateurs, to the undifferentiated masses. Whether he identifies himself with the Good and with divine Perfection, with the Beautiful or the True, a clerk is always on the side of the oppressors. A watchdog or a jester: it is up to him to choose.

M. Benda has chosen the cap and bells and M. Marcel the kennel; they have the right to do so, but if literature is one day to be able to enjoy its essence, the writer, without class, without colleges, without salons, without excess of honors, and without indignity, will be thrown into the world, among men, and the very notion of clerkship will appear inconceivable. The spiritual, moreover, always rests upon an ideology, and ideologies are freedom when they make themselves and oppression when they are made. The writer who has attained full self-consciousness will therefore not make himself the guardian of any spiritual hero; he will no longer know the centrifugal movement whereby certain of his predecessors turned their eyes away from the world to contemplate the heaven of established values; he will know that his job is not adoration of the spiritual, but rather spiritualization.

Spiritualization, that is, *renewal*. And there is nothing else to spiritualize, nothing else to renew but this multicolored and concrete world with its weight, its opaqueness, its zones of generalisation, and its swarm of anecdotes, and that invincible Evil which gnaws at it without ever being able to destroy it. The writer will renew it as is, the raw, sweaty, smelly, everyday world, in order to submit it to freedoms on the foundation of a freedom. Literature in this classless society would thus be the world aware of itself, suspended in a free act, and offering itself to the free judgment of all men, the reflective self-awareness of a classless society. It is by means of the book that the members of this society would be able to get their bearings, to see themselves and see their situation. But as the portrait compromises the model, as the simple presentation is already the beginning of change, as the work of art, taken in the totality of its exigencies, is not a simple description of the present but a judgment of this present in the name of a future, finally, as every book contains an appeal, this awareness of self is a surpassing of self. The universe is not contested in the name of simple consumption, but in the name of the hopes and sufferings of those who inhabit it. Thus, concrete literature will be a synthesis of Negativity, as a power of uprooting from the given, and a Project, as an outline of a future order; it will be the Festival, the flaming mirror which burns everything reflected in it, and generosity, that is, a free invention, a gift. But if it is to be able to ally these two complementary aspects of freedom, it is not enough to accord the writer freedom to say everything; he must write for a public which has the freedom of changing everything; which means, besides suppression of classes, abolition of all dictatorship, constant renewal of frameworks, and the continuous overthrowing of order once it tends to congeal. In short, literature is, in essence, the subjectivity of a society in permanent revolution. In such a society it would go beyond the antinomy of word and action. Certainly in no case would it be regarded as an act; it is false to say that the author *acts* upon his readers; he merely makes an appeal to their freedom, and in order for his works to have any effect, it is necessary for the public to adopt them on their own account by an unconditioned decision. But in a collectivity which constantly corrects, judges, and metamorphoses itself, the written work can be an essential condition of action, that is, the moment of reflective consciousness.

Thus, in a society without classes, without dictatorship, and without stability, literature would end by becoming conscious of itself; it would understand that form and content, public and subject, are identical, that the formal freedom of saying and the material freedom of doing complete each other, and that one should be used to demand the other, that it best manifests the subjectivity of the person when it translates most deeply collective needs and, reciprocally, that its function is to express the concrete universal to the concrete universal and that its end is to appeal to the freedom of men so that they may realize and maintain the reign of human freedom. To be sure, this is utopian. It is possible to conceive this society, but we have no practical means at our disposal of realizing it. It has allowed us to perceive the conditions under which literature might manifest itself in its fullness and purity.

Printed in the United States
65075LVS00002B/61-75